TRIBUTARIES

*Essays & Verses Flowing From
& Celebrating Favorite Poems*

Kurt Luchs

© 2025 by Kurt Luchs

All Rights Reserved.

Set in Adobe Garamond with LaTeX.

Robert Bly, "Hunting Pheasants in a Cornfield" from *Silence in the Snowy Fields*. Copyright © 1962 by Robert Bly. Published by Wesleyan University Press. Used by permission.

Jorge Luis Borges, "A Minor Poet" from "Fifteen Coins," translated by Alastair Reid, from *The Gold of the Tigers: Selected Later Poems*. Copyright © 1972, 1975 by Emece Editores, S.A., Buenos Aires. Translation copyright © 1976, 1977 by Alastair Reid. Used by permission of Penguin Books, an imprint of Penguin Publishing Group, a division of Penguin Random House, LLC. All rights reserved.

Lucille Clifton, "the message of crazy horse" from *Collected Poems of Lucille Clifton*. Copyright © 1987 by Lucille Clifton. Reprinted with the permission of The Permissions Company, LLC on behalf of BOA Editions, Ltd., boaeditions.org.

Louise Glück, "Mother and Child" from *The Seven Ages*. Copyright © 2001 by Louise Glück. Used by permission of HarperCollins Publishers.

Homer, excerpt from Book 22 "Bloodshed" from *The Odyssey*, translated by Emily Wilson. Copyright © 2017 by Emily Wilson. Used by permission of W. W. Norton & Company, Inc.

David Ignatow, "For My Daughter" from *Against the Evidence: Selected Poems 1934-1994*. Copyright © 1994 by David Ignatow. Published by Wesleyan University Press. Used by permission.

Etheridge Knight, "Feeling Fucked Up" from *The Essential Etheridge Knight*. Copyright © 1986 by Etheridge Knight. Reprinted by permission of University of Pittsburgh Press.

Kenneth Koch, "Fresh Air" from *On the Great Atlantic Rainway: Selected Poems 1959-1988*. Copyright © 1962 by Kenneth Koch. Used by permission of Alfred A. Knopf, an imprint of the Knopf, Doubleday Publishing Group, a division of Random House, LLC. All rights reserved.

Philip Larkin, "Annus mirabilis" from *Complete Poems*, edited by Archie Burnett Copyright © 2012 by the Estate of Philip Larkin. Reprinted by permission of Farrar, Straus & Giroux, LLC. All rights reserved.

D. H. Lawrence, "The Ship of Death" from *The Complete Poems of D. H. Lawrence*, edited by V. De Sola Pinto and F. W. Roberts. Copyright © 1964, 1971 by Angelo Ravagli and C. M. Weekley, Executors of the Estate of Frieda Lawrence Ravagli. Used by permission of Penguin Books, an imprint of Penguin Publishing Group, a division of Penguin Random House, LLC. All rights reserved.

Federico Garcia Lorca, "Home from a Walk," translated by Robert Bly, from *Lorca & Jimenez: Selected Poems*. Copyright © 1973, 1997 by Robert Bly, © 1967 by Sixties Press. Reprinted with permission from Beacon Press, Boston, Massachusetts.

Gabriela Mistral, "Slow Rain" aka "La Lluvia Lenta," translated by H. R. Hays, from *Poetry* (May 1943). Reprinted with the permission of the Estate of H. R. Hays.

Mary Oliver, "Bone" from *Why I Wake Early*. Reprinted by the permission of The Charlotte Sheedy Literary Agency as agent for the author. Copyright © 2004, 2005, 2017 by Mary Oliver with permission of Bill Reichblum.

Charles Simic, "Evening" from *Selected Poems 1963-1983*. Copyright © 1971 by Charles Simic. Reprinted with the permission of George Braziller, Inc. (New York), www.georgebraziller.com. All rights reserved.

Wislawa Szymborska, "Possibilities," translated by Clare Cavanagh and Stanislaw Baranczak, from *Poems New and Collected*. Copyright © by The Wislawa Szymborska Foundation. English language copyright © 1998 by HarperCollins Publishers. Used by permission of HarperCollins Publishers.

James Tate, "Poem to Some of My Recent Poems" from *Selected Poems*. Copyright © 1991 by James Tate. Published by Wesleyan University Press. Used by permission.

ISBN: 978-1-963846-47-8 (paperback)
Library of Congress Control Number: 2025943028

Sagging Meniscus Press
Montclair, New Jersey
saggingmeniscus.com

*In memory of my mother
and my fifth grade teacher Mrs. Francis,
who first taught me to love and understand poetry.*

Contents

Introduction   xi

WALLACE STEVENS
"Of Mere Being," by Wallace Stevens   2
Merely Being Wallace Stevens   3
Of "Of Mere Being"   6

ROBINSON JEFFERS
"To the Stone-cutters," by Robinson Jeffers   8
Robinson Jeffers, Stone-cutter of Tor House   9
To "To the Stone-cutters"   12

DAVID IGNATOW
"For My Daughter," by David Ignatow   14
Choose a Star: David Ignatow and the Power of Plain Speaking   15
For My Daughters   17

PHILIP LARKIN
"Annus Mirabilis," by Philip Larkin   20
The Remarkable Year: Philip Larkin Looks Back on Sex   21
1964   24

D.H. LAWRENCE
"The Ship of Death," by D.H. Lawrence   26
All Aboard! D. H. Lawrence and "The Ship of Death"   30
The Canoe of Death   34

ETHERIDGE KNIGHT
"Feeling Fucked Up," by Etheridge Knight   38
Swearing On His Life: Etheridge Knight in the Prison of Loneliness   39
Hit and Run   43
Crime Prevention in Wheaton, Illinois   45

WISLAWA SZYMBORSKA

"Possibilities," by Wislawa Szymborska (translated by Clare Cavanaugh
    and Stanislaw Baranczak)   *48*
The Highly Improbable Wislawa Szymborska   *50*
Impossibilities   *54*

LUCILLE CLIFTON

"the message of crazy horse," by Lucille Clifton   *58*
From One American Original to Another: Lucille Clifton on Crazy Horse   *59*
Near Death   *64*

GABRIELA MISTRAL

"Slow Rain *[first version]*," by Gabriela Mistral (translated by H. R. Hays)   *68*
The Mystery of Gabriela Mistral   *70*
Wasted Years   *76*

H. D.

"Evening," by H. D.   *78*
The Ever-Changing Images of H. D.   *79*
Not Quite Awake   *84*

JORGE LUIS BORGES

"A Minor Poet," by Jorge Luis Borges (translated by Alastair Reid)   *86*
Ah, Did You Once See Borges Plain?   *87*
Another Minor Poet   *92*
What Borges Said   *93*

FEDERICO GARCIA LORCA

"Home from a Walk," by Federico Garcia Lorca (translated by Robert Bly)   *96*
Lorca in the City That Never Sleeps   *97*
Migration   *103*

MARY OLIVER

"Bone," by Mary Oliver   *106*
Mary Oliver, Mary Oliver   *108*
Cottonwood Seeds   *112*

LEWIS CARROLL

"Jabberwocky," by Lewis Carroll — *114*
Here We Come A-Lewis Carrolling, or: Some Sensible Thoughts
    on the Nonsense of "Jabberwocky" — *115*
A Nonsense Verse — *120*
A Literary Limerick — *121*

KENNETH KOCH

"Fresh Air," by Kenneth Koch — *124*
Still Fresh and Funny After All These Years: The Enduring Subversive
    Charm of Kenneth Koch's Biggest and Most Serious Joke — *131*
A Villanelle for Kenneth — *140*

HOMER

"The Odyssey: Excerpt from Book 22: "Bloodshed"," by Homer (translated
    by Emily Wilson) — *142*
Found in Translation: Homer Through the Eyes of Emily Wilson — *143*
The Sign of Odysseus — *149*

LOUISE GLÜCK

"Mother and Child," by Louise Glück — *152*
Maternal and Eternal Mysteries: The Interrogations of Louise Glück — *153*
To My Chinese Daughters — *158*

ROBERT BLY

"Hunting Pheasants in a Cornfield," by Robert Bly — *162*
Hunting Everything but Pheasants with Robert Bly — *163*
The Boulder — *169*

CHARLES SIMIC

"Evening [first version]," by Charles Simic — *172*
Listening to the Grass and to Charles Simic — *173*
Mr. Monotonous — *177*

JAMES TATE
"Poem to Some of My Recent Poems," by James Tate   180
James Tate and the Saving Grace of Poetic Narrative   181
Love Poem to My Love Poems   187

Afterword   191
Acknowledgements   195

TRIBUTARIES

Introduction

Every writer starts as a reader. That's what first drew me into writing poetry—a fascination with its music, its magic, its mystery and its power to move me emotionally, intellectually and spiritually. I wanted very much to learn how to do that! Of course, one learns an art in two ways: by doing, and by studying worthy examples. Thus began a lifelong habit of thinking about and analyzing some of my favorite poems.

Only recently did it occur to me that there might be some value in publishing essays like these. Not academic treatises, which have their own dry, dusty value, I'm sure, but rather personal notes without any ax to grind other than increasing understanding and enjoyment. Further, I felt there was room for something new in the realm of literary appreciation, a double-pronged tribute that included both an essay and an ekphrastic poem of my own, either about or in response to or inspired by or somehow akin to the poems I was looking at. I think this might constitute one of those hybrid forms I keep hearing about.

Needless to say (but I'll say it anyway), I have no illusions that the tribute poems put me in the company of the authors I write about. They are simply another way of responding to some works of literature that I truly admire and that I would like to think have shaped me and my writing.

All of these "tributaries," as I have dubbed them, have appeared or will appear in the quarterly journal *Exacting Clam*. I plan to keep producing them indefinitely, as the number of poems I hope to examine and praise in both prose and verse is endless. If you don't see your favorite poem here, keep reading. It may well show up eventually.

WALLACE STEVENS

Of Mere Being

By Wallace Stevens

The palm at the end of the mind,
Beyond the last thought, rises
In the bronze decor,

A gold-feathered bird
Sings in the palm, without human meaning,
Without human feeling, a foreign song.

You know then that it is not the reason
That makes us happy or unhappy.
The bird sings. Its feathers shine.

The palm stands on the edge of space.
The wind moves slowly in the branches.
The bird's fire-fangled feathers dangle down.

MERELY BEING WALLACE STEVENS

The first time I read "Of Mere Being" by Wallace Stevens, I knew I had to memorize it. I could not proceed without this poem as part of my permanent mental furniture. No one but Stevens could have written it. In fact it's a tiny distillation of his lifelong mannerisms and obsessions into one concentrated dose, at twelve lines even shorter and more potent than a sonnet.

The exact date of composition is unknown, but most likely sometime in 1955, the last year of his life. One is therefore tempted, somewhat irrationally yet irresistibly, to view it as a summary or closing argument. Apparently Holly Stevens felt that way. When she edited a volume of her father's selected poetry in 1971, she titled it after the first line of this poem, *The Palm at the End of the Mind*, and gave it pride of place as the final poem in the book.

The title of the poem could serve as easily for a book of metaphysics or an essay by Francis Bacon, which is typical Wallace Stevens. He puts his philosophical preoccupations front and center. When originally published in *Opus Posthumous* in 1957, the last word of the first three-line stanza was "distance." Holly Stevens changed it back to the word used in the typescript draft, "decor." And that is a better word, such a Wallace Stevens word! Of course at the end of his mind there would still be something describable as a decor and of course it would be bronze. Could this be the "bric-a-brac" that Robert Frost supposedly accused him of writing about?

The second stanza introduces the key image: "A gold-feathered bird / Sings in the palm, without human meaning, / Without human feeling, a foreign song." The movement from bronze to gold subtly suggests being ushered into the presence of majesty. There the mind stops in its tracks, transfixed. What lies at the end of the mind, beyond the last thought, is a vision all the more compelling because it simply bypasses the intellect, making itself known only to direct apprehension. Suddenly the "mere being" of the title takes on new weight. Stevens plays on both of the main meanings of "mere," as in "smallest or slightest," and also "pure." In the former sense, ordinary, unexpanded consciousness (a "reducing valve," as Aldous Huxley called it) presents some everyday sensory data to us and reason steps in to analyze and interpret. In the latter sense, though, "mere being," pure being, cannot be interpreted by reason.

Thus the powerful realization that opens stanza three: "You know then that it is not the reason / That makes us happy or unhappy." The first two stanzas consist of a single sentence flowing smoothly like a film. The final two stanzas consist of six sentences, more like a quick succession of still photographs. The last line of stanza three contains two uncharacteristically concise sentences of three words each: "The bird sings. Its feathers shine." We can almost picture the poet's mouth agape with wonder. He's already told us the bird is singing. The reiteration has a bit of a hypnotic effect, or hints that the poet himself is under some kind of spell, perhaps his own.

The fourth and final stanza builds on everything that has come before. In a way it recapitulates the structure of the entire poem. It's a fractal, self-similar to the whole. First we notice the palm, which "stands on the edge of space." What space? Where? Let's leave those questions for the moment. In the second line we perceive something in the palm, but not yet the bird: "The wind moves slowly in the branches." Note that Stevens doesn't focus on the movement of the branches, but rather on what is making them move. He intuits the invisible by means of the visible. Because of this, and because wind is frequently used in religious literature as a metaphor for the spirit, this line is often taken to refer to a movement of the spirit. I believe this reading is correct.

The last line of the poem takes us by surprise, because up until that point Stevens doesn't employ a lot of the usual poetic devices. It's all imagery and plain talk. Only in this line does he overtly use alliteration and internal rhyme: "The bird's fire-fangled feathers dangle down." Obviously "fire-fangled" is the centerpiece of this line. According to the Oxford English Dictionary there are more than 171,476 words currently in use in the English language, and another 47,156 obsolete words. Like Shakespeare, however, Stevens did not find that to be quite enough for his purposes, so he invented one. The neologism "fire-fangled" conveys the meaning of "decked out," especially in a foppish manner, as well as the more archaic root meaning of "a silly or fantastic contrivance" (see Merriam-Webster).

With this melodious line the speech of the poem becomes a song of praise and awe.

Naturally, Stevens being Stevens, and poetry being poetry, there are layers in this thing. The poem implies many questions, giving no answers but itself. Can we ever perceive reality directly? And if we could, what difference would that make in our understanding of it? If we are forever trapped in our own heads, is that internal universe any smaller or less mysterious or complex than the one around us? What if any is the relation between the two?

Like other Stevens poems-about-poetry, "Of Mere Being" both explores and enacts these unspoken yet very present questions. Whether space (external or internal) can have an edge, and whether anything lies beyond that, the poet encompasses all of it, planting a palm with a dazzling unknown bird in its branches to mark the occasion. He transmutes reason's wandering and wondering into primal wonder.

Of "Of Mere Being"

Near the end, the poet sings of a palm
and a mysterious bird made of fire,
both just beyond the reach of his rational mind,

a mind that deals as readily with the duties
of an insurance executive as with
the astonishment of being Wallace Stevens.

Is the strange image of his own making
or is it a final gift from the universe
to its most ardent and articulate admirer?

Either way, he is transfixed with awe, we feel it
in the shortening sentences and the pure wonderment
of the music that emerges only in the last, lovely, unlikely line.

ROBINSON JEFFERS

To the Stone-cutters

By Robinson Jeffers

Stone-cutters fighting time with marble, you foredefeated
Challengers of oblivion
Eat cynical earnings, knowing rock splits, records fall down,
The square-limbed Roman letters
Scale in the thaws, wear in the rain. The poet as well
Builds his monument mockingly;
For man will be blotted out, the blithe earth die, the brave sun
Die blind and blacken to the heart:
Yet stones have stood for a thousand years, and pained thoughts found
The honey of peace in old poems.

ROBINSON JEFFERS, STONE-CUTTER OF TOR HOUSE

Robinson Jeffers' reputation plummeted during the latter part of his life, mostly because of his political beliefs regarding World War II. He strongly opposed U.S. entry into the conflict. Whether his stance was justified or not, it was principled, and it's worth noting that the "Good War" resulted in the greatest slaughter in human history, the first—and so far only—use of nuclear weapons in wartime, the firebombing of Dresden and Tokyo, and the enslavement of 100 million East Europeans under Soviet communism, not to mention the millions of Russian soldiers who wound up in Soviet gulags for the crime of having briefly glimpsed the freedom of the West during their war service. And that's on top of Hitler's boundless atrocities, which of course started it all.

Jeffers kept on writing but his literary standing did not begin to recover until several years after his death in 1962, when his work was championed by the emerging environmental movement. The now-defunct organization Friends of the Earth even named their publication *Not Man Apart* after a phrase from a Jeffers poem. In 1992 Robert Hass edited a volume called *Rock and Hawk: Selected Shorter Poems by Robinson Jeffers*, which did a lot to bring the poet back into prominence. "To the Stone-Cutters" was included in that collection. It has always been one of Jeffers' most anthologized poems.

At first glance, it's hard to explain the poem's ability to lodge itself so firmly in our consciousness. It appears to be—no, it actually is—a rather straightforward statement of an obvious truth, that no human creation lasts forever. We return to the earth, and eventually so does everything we have made. And yet we keep creating, in futile defiance of entropy. Why? And how does a ten-line poem on this subject have more staying power than most, becoming the exception that proves the rule?

Like his contemporary Marianne Moore, Jeffers made little or no place for conventional metrics in his verse. He didn't believe they were essential, and Jeffers is above all else a poet of essentials. His sonorous phrases seem inspired in equal parts by the King James Bible and the ancient Greeks who were his lifelong companions.

His chief compositional technique here is alliteration, the oldest trick in the book, even older than rhyme. However, he often uses it in a sophisticated way. In the first line, for example: "Stone-cutters fighting time with marble, you foredefeated . . ." there is the "t" sound in "Stone-cutters fighting time" and the "f" sound in "fighting" and "foredefeated." The latter two words include both sounds and thus link the respective phrases more closely.

Lines two through five offer a harvest of "n," "r" and "l" sounds: "Challengers of oblivion / Eat cynical earnings, knowing rock splits, records fall down, / The square-limbed Roman letters / Scale in the thaws, wear in the rain." I probably can't defend the thought rationally, but to my ear this flood of soft consonants reenacts the sense of the elements wearing down the stone.

The transition from the end of line five to line six brings more soft consonant alliteration, this time with an "m" sound: "The poet as well builds his monument mockingly;" it also sets up the climax and coda of the poem, both of which use hard consonant alliteration. The climactic lines are seven and eight: "For man will be blotted out, the blithe earth die, the brave sun / Die blind and blacken to the heart". Five "b's" in two lines, almost like hammer blows. The "m" in "man" also connects it to the previous line. The images and sounds vividly convey the poem's central theme that all things must pass.

Interestingly, when the poem was first published in a magazine, the eighth line was slightly different: "Die blind, his heart blackening:". By the time the poem was collected into *Tamar and Other Poems*, the line had been given its current, much more memorable and powerful form. It's an object lesson in the importance of revision. In this case, changing a single line arguably turned a good poem into a great one.

The coda, lines nine and ten, is less a rebuttal to the climactic lines than Jeffers' statement of faith that art matters because it extends us beyond ourselves and because it offers comfort in the face of inevitable loss: "Yet stones have stood for a thousand years, and pained thoughts found / The honey of peace in old poems." The hard "st" sounds of "stones" and "stood" add emphasis, as do the hard "p's" of "pained," "peace" and "poems," as well as hearkening back to the "poet" in line five. Again, in Jeffers' hands, alliteration can be both obvious and subtle.

Here's a question: Why does he make his stone-cutters the builders of monuments—gravestones—instead of, say, sculptors? Don't sculptors also fight time with marble? Well, yes, they do. I think the author's choice here means to remind us that poetry (the explicit parallel to stone-cutting) can be simultaneously high art and humble craft. Not every town has a statue, but every town has a graveyard. Thanks to Jeffers' masterful use of limited poetic means, this little work with a big heart is now one of those old poems in which our pained thoughts can find the honey of peace.

To "To the Stone-cutters"

"Stones have stood for a thousand years," you said,
and this little one of yours, cut from the hard marble
of our beloved Anglo-Saxon, has already made it
into its second century. I think it will live
as long as there are humans left on earth
who remember what it is to be human,
a future you did not consider very likely,
though if it should come to pass
your tough and tender poems will have played their part.
How often you spoke of our end,
sometimes almost with relish, other times with regret.
You foresaw an age when the hawks and sea lions
would own the rocky California coast without the eye of man or woman
to recognize their majesty and celebrate it in words musical and true.
I hope you're wrong. And in your huge, hurt heart—
the heart of many a misunderstood misanthropist—
I believe you hoped so too.
"The poet as well builds his monument mockingly," you said,
but all you ever mocked was the imbecility of politics
and the madness of war, two sides of the same counterfeit coin.
For the stone-cutters, your brothers and sisters
in the twin arts of nobility and futility, you felt nothing
but love, the same love that welled up in you like ocean waves
for the whole wide woebegone world.

DAVID IGNATOW

For My Daughter

By David Ignatow

When I die choose a star
and name it after me
that you may know
I have not abandoned
or forgotten you.
You were such a star to me,
following you through birth
and childhood, my hand
in your hand.

When I die
choose a star and name it
after me so that I may shine
down on you, until you join
me in darkness and silence
together.

CHOOSE A STAR: DAVID IGNATOW AND THE POWER OF PLAIN SPEAKING

There are writers we love as readers, for the enjoyment they give us and their angle on the human experience; and there are writers we love as writers, for what they can teach us about our craft. Sometimes a writer is both things to us, but not always. While I enjoy T. S. Eliot and Ezra Pound, in moderation, for various reasons that don't bear going into here, they could never serve as models for me to follow, in art or (heaven help me) in life.

Ever since I first encountered David Ignatow's poetry in the early seventies, I have taken much from it as a reader and as a writer. He could be described as the love child of Walt Whitman and William Carlos Williams, with, as Robert Bly observed, a little Hemingway thrown in. His poems are almost always plain and unassuming, usually free verse, occasionally prose poems, yet they pack a powerful sucker punch that sneaks up on you. This is all the more remarkable in that, as James Dickey wrote in an early review, "Ignatow does almost completely without the traditional skills of English versification." In the right hands, apparently, no technique is also a technique.

The poem I want to discuss here, "For My Daughter," is quite short, only fifteen lines, three simple sentences, two stanzas. It dates from the sixties and did not find its way into a book until Ignatow's first collected volume, *Poems 1934–1969* (Wesleyan, 1970). Judging by how many web sites it appears on today, it must be one of his best-loved works. It begins:

> When I die choose a star
> and name it after me
> that you may know
> I have not abandoned
> or forgotten you.

Official practice would be to put commas after "die" and "me." The more sensible practice adopted by Ignatow, regardless of rules, is to avoid punctuation except where the lack of it would leave the passage less clear.

Poets should trust their instincts and the intelligence of their readers. His line breaks in this sentence do the work of punctuation, and the run-on first line has the effect of leaping past the idea of his mortality right into how his daughter can begin to handle it. We infer that, just as he is now introducing her to death, he once introduced her to stargazing, an age-old father-daughter pastime. Note how quickly and effortlessly he has made the personal universal. What father has not wondered how to have this conversation with his children? And who else but Ignatow would be so disarmingly direct yet gentle?

The second sentence amplifies and inverts this thought: "You were such a star to me, / following you through birth / and childhood, my hand / in your hand." Did you catch that? He's not holding her hand in his, he's letting her hold his hand in hers, a subtle but meaningful difference, and part of the quiet brilliance of this poem. It is the natural order of things for the caregiver to become the one needing care, and for the child to become the parent. Natural or not, though, it is a painful reality that is difficult to face, and from the beginning he intends to help his daughter do that.

The third and final sentence also functions as the second stanza. It starts by repeating the first two lines of the poem, breaking them a little differently so that the whole stanza has some of the run-on feeling of the first line, for heightened anticipation. By the time we get to the last four lines we are nearly ready for the emotional weight that the poem has accumulated:

> . . . so that I may shine
> down on you, until you join
> me in darkness and silence
> together.

And that, ladies and gentlemen, is how you talk to your daughter about death, yours and hers and everyone's. Small wonder that James Wright titled his essay about Ignatow "A Plain Brave Music" (see Wright's *Collected Prose*, The University of Michigan Press, 1983).

David Ignatow was born in 1914, the same year as another fine American poet, Randall Jarrell, but outlived his contemporary by thirty-two years, producing several dozen books of verse. Jarrell died in 1965, and only four years later his *Complete Poems* was in print. I can hardly believe that Ignatow died in 1997, almost a quarter of a century ago, and we are still waiting for his *Complete Poems*. I would make a special plea to Wesleyan University Press, which holds the rights to many of his books, and to the Library of America, which specializes in such projects, to put all of Ignatow's work within easy reach of poetry lovers in his country. It is not too much to ask for this most American of poets.

For My Daughters

When you scatter my ashes in Northside Park
many years from now (I hope,
though we have no say in these things),
let the wind take them and become
my voice, invisible, a wordless song
known only by its singular note
and its ability to make leaves and branches
dance like little green puppets
for your pleasure and amusement.
After the leaves have stilled and hushed,
the wind that is me will have moved
into the echo chamber of memory
where endings try so hard not to end.
Yet every song must have an ending.
I thought I knew what joy was
before you came to me. I doubt I will know
what grief is until I must say goodbye.
I would rather let the wind say it for me,
and the long brown grasses on the shore
of the pond where we looked for turtles together,
and the water rippling with tiny waves
carried beyond themselves
into the darkening dusk.

PHILIP LARKIN

Annus Mirabilis

By Philip Larkin

Sexual intercourse began
In nineteen sixty-three
(which was rather late for me)—
Between the end of the Chatterley ban
And the Beatles' first LP.

Up to then there'd only been
A sort of bargaining,
A wrangle for the ring,
A shame that started at sixteen
And spread to everything.

Then all at once the quarrel sank:
Everyone felt the same,
And every life became
A brilliant breaking of the bank,
A quite unlosable game.

So life was never better than
In nineteen sixty-three
(Though just too late for me)—
Between the end of the Chatterley ban
And the Beatles' first LP.

THE REMARKABLE YEAR: PHILIP LARKIN LOOKS BACK ON SEX

T. S. Eliot once voiced the opinion that the best poet to write in English in the last 200 years was W. B. Yeats. Although Old Possum was wrong about many things, I believe he was right about that. Which leads us to the follow-up question: Who is the best poet to write in our language since Yeats? We might have to answer that in two parts, depending on which side of the Atlantic Ocean we're talking about (two peoples separated by a common language and all that). In America, I'd say possibly James Wright, possibly W. S. Merwin, possibly Louise Glück. In the U.K., I think it's either Ted Hughes or Philip Larkin, a pair of polar opposites. For my money, Hughes edges out Larkin, but there's no denying the strength and durability of Larkin's achievement.

As one of the primary apostles of formalism, he helped drag rhythm and rhyme kicking and screaming into the latter half of the twentieth century. The trick is always to fit ordinary speech comfortably within formal constraints, with thoughts, images and turns of phrase so arranged as to be meaningful and memorable. Easy peasey! Larkin is a poet of the everyday, seeking illumination in the quotidian. More often than not, he finds what he's seeking. Many of his poems are now justly regarded as classics.

The poem we're looking at today, "Annus Mirabilis," was written in June 1967 and seven years later became part of the final volume published during his lifetime, *High Windows* (1974). In it he looks back nostalgically on the beginnings of the sexual revolution, only a few years old at the time of writing, but it must have seemed like centuries, so vast were the social and cultural changes the decade had wrought. How appropriate that this poem should be one of the first to mention the Beatles, seeing as they had led and come to symbolize those changes (Allen Ginsberg's "Portland Coliseum" from 1965 mentions the group members by name but not the group itself).

I'm guessing it's no accident that the manuscript bears a date of June 16, 1967, exactly three weeks after the release of *Sgt. Pepper's Lonely Hearts Club*

Band. That the Beatles were doing work of lasting value had been apparent since at least 1965 to open-minded listeners from the worlds of jazz and classical music, including Miles Davis and Leonard Bernstein, among many others. However, *Sgt. Pepper* was the turning point that caused every culture critic to take them seriously. When Larkin wrote "Annus Mirabilis" he could feel confident that name-checking them would not make the poem seem hopelessly dated someday.

The poem is twenty lines long, consisting of four stanzas of five lines each, employing a rhyme scheme of ABBAB. The meter is mostly iambic, with plenty of exceptions. The first stanza neatly sets the scene:

Sexual intercourse began
In nineteen sixty-three
(Which was rather late for me)—
Between the end of the Chatterly ban
And the Beatles' first LP.

The trial of Penguin Books under the Obscene Publications Act for publishing the unexpurgated edition of *Lady Chatterly's Lover* by D.H. Lawrence resulted in a "not guilty" verdict on November 2, 1960. That the author's worst book effectively rid Britain of literary censorship is about the only good thing one can say about it. Penguin should have been prosecuted for publishing a misshapen novel that managed to make sex both boring and mawkishly stupid. The Beatles' first album, *Please Please Me*, came out March 23, 1963. Between and around the two dates singled out by Larkin fell two other events worth noting in regard to the sexual revolution. On December 4, 1961, birth control pills became available through the National Health Service, though until 1967 they were only given to married women. And in the summer of 1963, the Profumo scandal broke open.

That's the backdrop. The only use of first-person in the poem occurs in the parentheses in stanzas one and four, windows into Larkin's own view of these events. Why, one wonders, does he feel that the sexual revolution was "rather late for me"? Because he turned forty-one in 1963? Even before the advent of ED drugs, middle-aged people embraced the new sexual ethic as eagerly as the young. More so, perhaps, because they knew all too well what they had missed growing up.

That, in fact, is the subject of stanza two, where he recounts the old order, in which sex is "A sort of bargaining, / A wrangle for a ring, / A shame that started at sixteen / And spread to everything." To sum up the institution of marriage as "A wrangle for a ring" is profoundly dismissive and reductionist. And yet, from the young man's point of view, maybe not so far off. How insightful of Donald Davie to call him a poet of "lowered sights and diminished expectations." Larkin went through a pronounced Auden-worshipping phase when he was learning how to write, and this stanza does display some of Auden's genius for generalization.

Stanza three tells how things have been since the sexual revolution, which quickly produced "A brilliant breaking of the bank, / A quite unlosable game." Happiness all around, it would seem. Yet stanza four concludes the tale almost exactly as it began, on a note of irony mixed with poignant regret:

> So life was never better than
> In nineteen sixty-three
> (Though just too late for me)—
> Between the end of the Chatterly ban
> And the Beatles' first LP.

Treating the final stanza like the repetitive chorus of a pop song—shades of the Fab Four again—is a clever touch that drives home the underlying conflicted nature of the poem. If "life was never better," why does he have to keep saying that? Is he consciously echoing the song "Getting Better" from *Sgt. Pepper*, with the chorus that undercuts its own ostensible message, "It's getting better all the time (it can't get no worse)"? Yes, I think so. And here is a good place to leave off our examination of the poem, at the point where Larkin demonstrates that the sexual revolution was part of a bigger cultural tsunami that changed much more than sex, among other things causing high art and pop art to mate, blend into each other and became all but indistinguishable.

1964

They could do no wrong that year, no matter
What they set their hands to, it came out right.
Author Lennon proved mad as a hatter,
They conquered the world with "A Hard Day's Night"
(Movie, album *and* single) and they toured
Every stadium on the globe until
Their desire to play live was almost cured,
Except they still had contracts to fulfill.
The girls, the screams, the comic repartee
Must have blurred together as they rushed from
Studio to studio—BBC,
EMI, United Artists—pushed from
Limousines into humanity's arms
With no protection but their natural charms.

D.H. LAWRENCE

The Ship of Death

By D.H. Lawrence

I

Now it is autumn and the falling fruit
and the long journey towards oblivion.

The apples falling like great drops of dew
to bruise themselves an exit from themselves.

And it is time to go, to bid farewell
to one's own self, and find an exit
from the fallen self.

II

Have you built your ship of death, O have you?
O build your ship of death, for you will need it.

The grim frost is at hand, when the apples will fall
thick, almost thundrous, on the hardened earth.

And death is on the air like a smell of ashes!
Ah! can't you smell it?

And in the bruised body, the frightened soul
finds itself shrinking, wincing from the cold
that blows upon it through the orifices.

III

And can a man his own quietus make
with a bare bodkin?

With daggers, bodkins, bullets, man can make
a bruise or break of exit for his life;
but is that a quietus, O tell me, is it quietus?

Surely not so! for how could murder, even self-murder
ever a quietus make?

IV

O let us talk of quiet that we know,
that we can know, the deep and lovely quiet
of a strong heart at peace!

How can we this, our own quietus, make?

V

Build then the ship of death, for you must take
the longest journey, to oblivion.

And die the death, the long and painful death
that lies between the old self and the new.

Already our bodies are fallen, bruised, badly bruised,
already our souls are oozing through the exit
of the cruel bruise.

Already the dark and endless ocean of the end
is washing in through the breaches of our wounds,
already the flood is upon us.

Oh build your ship of death, your little ark
and furnish it with food, with little cakes, and wine
for the dark flight down oblivion.

VI

Piecemeal the body dies, and the timid soul
has her footing washed away, as the dark flood rises.

We are dying, we are dying, we are all of us dying
and nothing will stay the death-flood rising within us
and soon it will rise on the world, on the outside world.

We are dying, we are dying, piecemeal our bodies are dying
and our strength leaves us,
and our soul cowers naked in the dark rain over the flood,
cowering in the last branches of the tree of our life.

VII

We are dying, we are dying, so all we can do
is now to be willing to die, and to build the ship
of death to carry the soul on the longest journey.

A little ship, with oars and food
and little dishes, and all accoutrements
fitting and ready for the departing soul.

Now launch the small ship, now as the body dies
and life departs, launch out, the fragile soul
in the fragile ship of courage, the ark of faith
with its store of food and little cooking pans
and change of clothes,
upon the flood's black waste
upon the waters of the end
upon the sea of death, where still we sail
darkly, for we cannot steer, and have no port.

There is no port, there is nowhere to go
only the deepening black darkening still
blacker upon the soundless, ungurgling flood
darkness at one with darkness, up and down
and sideways utterly dark, so there is no direction any more
and the little ship is there; yet she is gone.
She is not seen, for there is nothing to see her by.
She is gone! gone! and yet
somewhere she is there.
Nowhere!

VIII

And everything is gone, the body is gone
completely under, gone, entirely gone.
The upper darkness is heavy as the lower,
between them the little ship

is gone
she is gone.

It is the end, it is oblivion.

IX

And yet out of eternity a thread
separates itself on the blackness,
a horizontal thread
that fumes a little with pallor upon the dark.

Is it illusion? or does the pallor fume
A little higher?
Ah wait, wait, for there's the dawn,
the cruel dawn of coming back to life
out of oblivion.

Wait, wait, the little ship
drifting, beneath the deathly ashy grey
of a flood-dawn.

Wait, wait! even so, a flush of yellow
and strangely, O chilled wan soul, a flush of rose.
A flush of rose, and the whole thing starts again.

X

The flood subsides, and the body, like a worn sea-shell
emerges strange and lovely.
And the little ship wings home, faltering and lapsing
on the pink flood,
and the frail soul steps out, into the house again
filling the heart with peace.

Swings the heart renewed with peace
even of oblivion.

Oh build your ship of death, oh build it!
for you will need it.
For the voyage of oblivion awaits you.

ALL ABOARD! D. H. LAWRENCE AND "THE SHIP OF DEATH"

D. H. Lawrence's poetic reputation has forever been overshadowed by his fame as a fiction writer, much like Thomas Hardy before him (though not all that much before him; it's odd to reflect that Hardy died in 1928, only two years before Lawrence, and that the bulk of Hardy's poetic production was contemporaneous with that of Lawrence, his junior by forty-five years). Yet I have always felt that his poems are superior to even the best of his novels, which of course are quite good, except for the ghastly *Lady Chatterley's Lover*.

Further, Lawrence's career as a poet prefigures those of some of the most talented poets in England and America several generations after him. I'm thinking of Ted Hughes, Sylvia Plath, James Wright, W. S. Merwin and Donald Hall, among others. Like Lawrence, each of these poets began by writing formal verse and then, compelled by the lure of new themes and new ways of thinking, as well as the spirit of the times, switched to free verse. In every case this change raised their work to a new level. The curious thing about Lawrence is that the transition from rhymes to free verse did not so much result in better work—he wrote great poems in both styles—but rather it was part of his lifelong quest to become ever more his true self, free of constraints and preconceptions.

Lawrence's journey of self-discovery ran parallel to his work and was fascinating both to him and to his friends and enemies. As Aldous Huxley noted, "Isn't it remarkable how everyone who knew Lawrence felt compelled to write about him?" Huxley's roman à clef *Point Counter Point* contains a character based on Lawrence, the fiery writer-artist-social critic Mark Rampion, and *Brave New World* is in many ways a reaction to the denatured dystopia that Huxley and Lawrence saw the world becoming.

"The Ship of Death" is certainly one of Lawrence's best poems, as well as the most famous. Not every writer knows when death is coming and has time and vitality enough to ponder it fruitfully. After years of suffering from tuberculosis, Lawrence finally began to succumb to it in the late 1920s. Before he died on March 2, 1930, he had given death a thorough going-over in a number of poems, most memorably in "Bavarian Gentians" and "The Ship of Death."

The latter poem is almost unique among poetic masterpieces in that it has no definitive version. While he had toiled through multiple drafts, some of them published separately, and the last version is the most complete, it is clearly unfinished. For example, in the beginning of the poem he starts some sentences with the poetic apostrophe "O," but at the middle and end he slips into the more workaday "Oh" for no apparent reason. Surely this minor inconsistency would've been cleaned up if he had lived.

That there is no definitive text of "The Ship of Death" may not matter as much as you might think, for several reasons. For one thing, though Lawrence was not a slapdash writer, he was also not a persnickety perfectionist, at least not in the sense of the poem as well-wrought-urn (see: Cleanth Brooks). As death approached, his idea of perfection had more to do with imaginative liberty and spontaneity, with capturing the moment. Then, too, this poem is about a journey into the unknown. It is in its nature to be open-ended and partially undefined.

The poem can be read as a liturgy for the dying, not unlike the *Tibetan Book of the Dead* or certain passages in the Anglican *Book of Common Prayer*. There are ten stanzas of varying lengths, each one a poem in its own right, and altogether adding up to something much more than the sum of its parts. In "The Ship of Death" as in nearly all of Lawrence's better free verse poems, the main poetic influence is not any of his predecessors or contemporaries. It is the King James Bible, especially the most explicitly poetic part of it, the Psalms. His sonorities, his imagery, and most of all his artful use of reiteration has its roots there.

Stanza I sets the scene and makes the autumnal mood official by using falling apples as a metaphor for death:

Now it is autumn and the falling fruit
and the long journey towards oblivion.

Already we can discern that this poem about death will be neither overly morbid nor sad. In fact, as we will see, despite some dark passages it is downright joyful. From the start he is treating death as part of the natural order. What's more, the death of a lone apple seems less tragic in that the tree from which it fell, the greater life, continues.

Stanza II brings the ship of death into it, although we have little idea at this point what the ship might be. Not a literal ship, at any rate, as it would be if the poem were two or three thousand years old and written about the death of a king instead of a modern everyman.

In Stanza III Lawrence takes a step sideways to deal with the issue of suicide. On the whole, he seems to be against it, "for how could murder, even self-murder / ever a quietus make?" It's worth noting that the author spent years dying from one of the most insidious diseases imaginable, but did not take his own life. No matter how painful, he viewed the death journey as sacrosanct, an essential human experience, not something to be dodged. The goal, he says in Stanza IV, is "a strong heart at peace." And here, I think, is his conception of the ship of death—a mental construct, a deep feeling, a final alignment of the best parts of the inner person.

This theme becomes more explicit in Stanza V, where he speaks of "the long and painful death / that lies between the old self and the new." That almost sounds like the Christian notion of death, yet he is careful in his verse, just as he was in his life, not to affiliate himself with any one tradition, preferring to borrow from them all to make his own. And when in the same stanza he writes, "Already the dark and endless ocean of the end / is washing in through the breaches of your wounds," it is a strangely inverted echo of the crucifixion, where instead of the wounds bleeding out, the waters of death bleed in through them. Very peculiar, and very much Lawrence.

Stanza VI is about the individual's fear of death, and also mentions his belief that human civilization is destroying itself in a collective death. The word is still out on that prophecy, though performing gain-of-function research on a deadly virus can't be a good sign.

Death finally comes for the Archbishop Lawrence in Stanza VII, and he says of the ship of death:

> She is gone! gone! and yet
> somewhere she is there.
> Nowhere!

The end? Not quite. While Stanza VIII affirms, "It is the end, it is oblivion," Stanza IX witnesses some kind of rebirth, "the cruel dawn of coming back to life / out of oblivion," and concludes with, "A flush of rose, and the whole thing starts again." That certainly appears to be an allusion to reincarnation. Once again, however, it would be hasty to attribute this to belief in anything as specific as Hinduism or Buddhism.

Stanza X reiterates the image of rebirth and finishes with a rousing exhortation nearly identical to the one that begins Stanza II:

> Oh build your ship of death, oh build it!
> for you will need it.
> For the voyage of oblivion awaits you.

Lawrence's ship of death metaphor is not quite like any other. It is not a ship set aflame to bury a Viking at sea, nor is it the boat in which Charon ferries the dead across the River Styx (or was that the River REO Speedwagon?). Like everything else he wrote, it is unique to him, and like the best of his work, it achieves universality. It started as his ship of death, but it's ours now. As Kenneth Rexroth writes in his Introduction to the *Selected Poems* published by New Directions, "*The Ship of Death* poems have an exaltation, a nobility, a steadiness, an insouciance, which is not only not of this time but which is rare in any time." Incidentally, though that volume is out of print, it's worth tracking down used, both for the quality of the selection and for Rexroth's essay, one of the best ever written about Lawrence.

The Canoe of Death

(With no apologies and a taffy apple to D. H. Lawrence.)

I.

Now it is Fall and the falling fruit
falls on me and sends me on the long journey towards oblivion.

Like swollen balls of dew they fall
down my shirt and briefs and seem to say, "No exit,"
but Jean-Paul Sartre used that already
and what is he but a fallen fruit?
Perhaps it is Springtime instead?
Anyway, it is time to look in the mirror
and wave bye-bye at one's self. So long!

II.

Have you carved your canoe of death, O tell me have you?
O you must carve your canoe of death,
I insist, really you must,
for they come in ever so handy when you are dead.
I've ridden in mine countless times.

But now Suzie Snowflake is nipping at my nose.
Was that thunder I heard, or . . . No, it was just another
apple that fell on my head. Silly me!
And death is on the air like an old cardigan sweater.
Dear me, can't you smell that nasty smell?
Someone is burning leaves.
And in the bruised apple, yes, the very same one
I told you about, the little worm is wriggling.
How tiny and cold he is!
There's a lesson there, don't you think?

III.

Quiet, please, O I beg you be quiet,
I can't hear myself think, it's such a tiny sound
like a dagger bruising a bare bodkin
or a bullet being bitten, O don't you see?
If you don't shut up I shall murder you. Ah!

IV.

(A minute of silence.)

V.

So build your canoe of death, you'll need it
where you're going, bye-bye, far away
where the sugar plums grow and never fall
nasty plop! on your head and make it all sticky
like a slimy nasty old worm. Ugh! O ugh I say!
Already something has soaked my breeches,
the waters of the infinite sea of boredom
are drenching my codpiece.

O carve your canoe of death, you witless twit,
stock it with tuna fish salad and candied apples
and powdered milk and sugarless gum—*anything*,
just so you go away
and don't come back.

VI.

We are dying, O please let us die dear God,
I won't forgive you if you don't
for we are dying bit by bit,
our noses are falling off,
I feel dead already, don't you?
O say that you do!

VII.

(A minute of quiet, bitter sobbing.)

VIII.

(Several minutes of uncontrolled weeping, followed by the Author falling to his hands and knees and banging his head on the floor.)

IX.

(The sobbing gradually becomes a violent, hacking cough.)

X.

Let us sail our little canoe through the lagoon of life,
let's see if we can sink it, shall we?
O dear God the doctor says I will live after all!
I threw an apple at him and he bruised beautifully.
Then he smiled and sank my boats in the bathtub.
I could have kissed him for joy.
But instead I held him under the suds
and started him on the long journey towards oblivion.

ETHERIDGE KNIGHT

Feeling Fucked Up

By Etheridge Knight

Lord she's gone done left me done packed / up and split
and I with no way to make her
come back and everywhere the world is bare
bright bone white   crystal sand glistens
dope death dead dying and jiving drove
her away made her take her laughter and her smiles
and her softness and her midnight sighs—

Fuck Coltrane and music and clouds drifting in the sky
fuck the sea and trees and the sky and birds
and alligators and all the animals that roam the earth
fuck marx and mao fuck fidel and nkrumah and
democracy and communism fuck smack and pot
and red ripe tomatoes fuck joseph fuck mary fuck
god jesus and all the disciples fuck fanon nixon
and malcolm fuck the revolution fuck freedom fuck
the whole muthafucking thing
all i want now is my woman back
so my soul can sing

Swearing on His Life: Etheridge Knight in the Prison of Loneliness

The poet and critic Malcom Cowley once referred to the writer Conrad Aiken as "the buried giant of American literature," a fair assessment to anyone familiar with Aiken's poetry, novels, short stories and autobiography. In a similar fashion, Etheridge Knight could be called the buried giant of the Black Arts Movement of the sixties and seventies. His work was recognized and celebrated during his lifetime, to be sure. And he is remembered today, with several of his poems attaining the stature of American classics, such as the much-anthologized "The Idea of Ancestry," "The Bones of My Father," and the one we'll be looking at here, "Feeling Fucked Up." Yet he is nowhere near as famous as other BAM luminaries, such as Maya Angelou and Nikki Giovanni and the founder of the movement, Amiri Baraka (aka Leroi Jones).

There are several reasons, none of them having anything to do with the quality of his work. He didn't start writing until he was in his thirties while serving a sentence for armed robbery. Before that he grew up in poverty in Mississippi and Kentucky, one of seven children. Despite reportedly being a brilliant student he dropped out of school in the eighth grade and immediately went to work. In 1947 he joined the Army where he served ten years, seeing battle in Korea and receiving a shrapnel wound that left him with chronic pain and a morphine habit that he would struggle with for most of his life. Engaging in robbery to feed his habit led him to prison. And there, after his initial rage cooled, he began to turn his life around. He studied. He read voraciously. He found an outlet in poetry and determined to become a great writer.

By the time of his release in 1968 he had achieved that goal, publishing his first book, *Poems from Prison*, which was widely praised inside and outside the Black literary community (Gwendolyn Brooks and Donald Hall were both fans, among many others). There followed more than two decades of writing and four further books before he died of lung cancer in 1991 at the age of fifty-nine. He had overcome much and accomplished much. But he started late and died relatively young, and that no doubt affected his reputation in the long run. His work is still not nearly as well-known as it should be. Another factor here is that more than three decades after his death Etheridge Knight has yet to see a *Collected Poems*. A selected volume called *The Essential Etheridge Knight* from 1986 comes the closest, although it is far from complete and contains nothing from his last five years. To borrow a phrase from the poem of his we're looking at today, that is fucked up. Somebody should do something about it.

"Feeling Fucked Up" is atypical of Knight in that he doesn't normally employ profanity. In this poem he drops a total of fourteen f-bombs, including the one in the title and the "mothafucking" near the end. Profanity is a strong spice, to be used sparingly most of the time. However, there are occasions when unleashing a stream of curses makes perfect sense. When you accidentally hit your thumb with a hammer. When another driver cuts you off in traffic. When your bare foot steps on something squishy and wet, and you realize your cat failed to make it to the box again. And when your lover leaves you.

It is this last circumstance, one familiar to nearly everybody, that Knight addresses in this poem. The poem is in free verse consisting of two stanzas, the first being seven lines long and the second being eleven lines. Aside from the title, all of the swearing occurs in the second stanza.

The first line of the poem establishes both the situation and the author's colloquial tone, drawing from the idiom of the blues: "Lord she's gone done left me done packed / up and split." That forward slash within the line is a technique Knight uses frequently. It can be read different ways depending on the context—perhaps an additional break within the line, or setting apart a certain phrase. Here I take it to imply two readings with one phrase: she packed up and split in one continuous motion, one memory; and also she packed up and then split, two separate actions, drawn out as they happen. The latter reading sounds as if the author watched her do both of these things, leading to the buildup of grief, pain and anger that fuels the second stanza.

The rest of stanza one immediately dives into sharp feelings of loss:

> . . . everywhere the world is bare
> bright bone white   crystal sand glistens

The extra spaces between "white" and "crystal" effectively underscore the emptiness of a beach scene that is still beautiful but lacking the only beauty that matters now, the one that is no longer there. Stanza one concludes with an increasingly anguished cry of despair that perfectly sets up the outburst that will follow in stanza two:

> dope death dead dying and jiving drove
> her away made her take her laughter and her smiles
> and her softness and her midnight sighs—

Note the hard alliteration of five words beginning with "d" in that fifth line of stanza one—three of them death words—and the three gentler words beginning with "s" in the last two lines of the stanza. These words contrast the man's angry guilt with the woman's innocent charms, more bitterly missed now than ever.

The distinction between her laughter and her smiles is a nice touch. The key thing in this part of the stanza, though, is his admitting to his ongoing drug problem and the dishonesty it entails, along with a death wish signaled by the triple pile-on of "death dead dying". Apparently, it took the loss of his lover to wring this confession out of him.

Then comes the epic profane rant of stanza two, starting with "Fuck Coltrane and music and clouds drifting in the sky / fuck the sea and trees and the sky and birds" (note that this forward slash, and every one used hereafter, was inserted by me to denote a line break). Somewhat counterintuitively, the movement of his rage goes from the particular to the universal: first the icon of Black creativity Coltrane, then all music; first clouds drifting in the sky, then the sky itself. So far all of the things cited are those normally associated with happiness and tranquility. The sea, which was merely implied by the image of a white sandy beach in stanza one, is explicitly told to fuck itself in stanza two, perhaps for not being able to provide its accustomed peace in this time of grievous loss. It's worth mentioning that Coltrane is the only proper name or proper noun capitalized in the entire poem, outranking Mary, Joseph, Jesus and the author himself, who uses a Cummings-style small "i".

Knight starts to switch it up in line three of this stanza (line ten of the poem overall) by listing alligators among those creatures that should get fucked. Alligators? Really? Up until this poem, the only thing that ever fucked an alligator was another alligator. Again moving from the specific to the universal, he follows the curse against alligators with "all the animals that roam the earth". Now the litany of things that should be fucked enters high gear with politics and ideology: "fuck marx and mao fuck fidel and nkrumah and / democracy and communism" (lines four and five of stanza two, lines eleven and twelve of the poem overall). He pauses to call out "smack and pot / and red ripe tomatoes" (!) before heading into the home stretch of his rant, from the beginning of line thirteen to the end of the poem:

> . . . fuck joseph fuck mary fuck
> god jesus and all the disciples fuck fanon nixon
> and malcolm fuck the revolution fuck freedom fuck
> the whole mothafucking thing
> all i want now is my woman back
> so my soul can sing

I remembered that Kwame Nkrumah was the first President of Ghana, but I had to look up Frantz Fanon, the French West Indian Marxist theorist of decolonization whose work must've been important to Knight. Juxtaposing his name with that of Richard Nixon is one of the few notes of humor in this otherwise bleak poem.

Throughout this work resonates the idea of loneliness as its own kind of prison. As noted in the study by Cassie Premo, Knight often focuses on "the theme of prisons imposed from without (slavery, racism, poverty, incarceration) and prisons from within (addiction, repetition of painful patterns) [which] are countered by the theme of freedom." Knight himself once said, "Ideas are not the source of poetry. For me, it's passion, heart and soul." Few more passionate and soulful poems about the prison of loneliness exist in our language. I believe this poem will have things to say to us about our shared humanity for a long time to come.

Hit and Run

Shit motherfucker you're murdering me!
I wanted to scream, and did,
but no one was there to hear
nor could they have heard
over the roar of his engine
and the whine of mine,
his 18-wheeler drifting into my VW Rabbit
as he drifted off to sleep,
no warning, no turn signal, no horn
on a rainy and foggy Chicago midnight.
His right front wheels
smashed into my left,
bouncing my car into the overpass guard rail
that had me trapped.

Goddamn motherfucking piece of shit!
I bellowed again and again
as the car twirled and slammed back
into his other wheels,
each one the mouth of a Great White
looking to swallow me whole
or drag me under the behemoth,
tearing off hubcaps and side mirrors
like chunks of silver flesh
too tasty to chew properly,
spinning madly, adding vertigo to terror.

Son of a motherfucking bitch!
I gasped as I hit the guard rail again,
rebounding into the truck wheels once more
and landing behind him in the center lane,
finally stopping at a forty-five-degree angle,
the radiator already steaming,
the car so totaled I had to crawl
out the back hatch on my hands and knees.

I stood there shaking, lightly whiplashed
but otherwise unhurt
and oh so glad to be alive, car be damned.

That motherfucking bastard of a truck driver
kept going (the cops caught him later)
and I didn't care one bit
because while the crash was happening
my life had flashed before my eyes
exactly as they say it does,
and it was not a good life,
not even enough to put on a tombstone.
In that instant my spirit
came out of hibernation
wide-eyed and blinking in astonishment.
So began an awakening
that continues to this day,
every morning since then an unbidden gift
from a mysterious stranger whose face
has yet to emerge from the fog
and the never-ending screech
of giant rubber wheels grinding metal.

Crime Prevention in Wheaton, Illinois

The kids from next door never knew
what hit them when they tried
to steal our bicycles,
all four of our geese came at them
out of the dark, a terror of beaks
and talons on beating wings,
a mingled shrieking of tough old birds
and tender young humans
that echoed up and down Darling Street
at eleven o'clock in the evening,
leaving us unable to sleep
but helpless with laughter.
It was the first informal civics lesson
for our new neighbors, refugees
and survivors from Castro's Cuba:
we Americans take our private property
seriously, so don't fuck with us
or the creatures that used to be
dinosaurs will tear you apart.
And from that day forward
we were the best of friends.

WISLAWA SZYMBORSKA

Possibilities

By Wislawa Szymborska

translated by Clare Cavanaugh and Stanislaw Baranczak

I prefer movies.
I prefer cats.
I prefer the oaks along the Warta.
I prefer Dickens to Dostoyevsky.
I prefer myself liking people
to myself loving mankind.
I prefer keeping a needle and thread on hand, just in case.
I prefer the color green.
I prefer not to maintain
that reason is to blame for everything.
I prefer exceptions.
I prefer to leave early.
I prefer talking to doctors about something else.
I prefer the old fine-lined illustrations.
I prefer the absurdity of writing poems to the absurdity of not writing
    poems.
I prefer, where love's concerned, nonspecific anniversaries
that can be celebrated every day.
I prefer moralists
who promise me nothing.
I prefer cunning kindness to the over-trustful kind.
I prefer the earth in civvies.
I prefer conquered to conquering countries.
I prefer having some reservations.
I prefer the hell of chaos to the hell of order.
I prefer Grimms' fairy tales to the newspapers' front pages.
I prefer leaves without flowers to flowers without leaves.
I prefer dogs with uncropped tails.
I prefer light eyes, since mine are dark.
I prefer desk drawers.
I prefer many things that I haven't mentioned here

to many things I've also left unsaid.
I prefer zeroes on the loose
to those lined up behind a cipher.
I prefer the time of insects to the time of stars.
I prefer to knock on wood.
I prefer not to ask how much longer and when.
I prefer keeping in mind even the possibility
that existence has its own reason for being.

THE HIGHLY IMPROBABLE WISLAWA SZYMBORSKA

British film historian Ian Christie has said of Alfred Hitchcock's troubled and still controversial film *Marnie*, "If you don't love *Marnie*, you don't love cinema." With equal justice it could be said, if you don't love Wislawa Szymborska, you don't love poetry. In fact, you don't love humanity, for whatever else she may be, she is the most human of poets. I am constantly running into people who say they don't read poetry, but they know and revere the work of Szymborska. I am sure it is her humanity that connects with these otherwise nonliterary readers.

Her star was slow to rise. Her road to the 1996 Nobel Prize in Literature was filled with stops, starts and detours. Born in 1923 in Prowent, Poland, by the time she was eight her family had moved to Krakow, where she spent the rest of her life.

After Hitler proved his complete lack of territorial ambitions by invading Poland in 1939 and starting World War II—thanks again, Neville Chamberlain—Szymborska's life, like that of every Pole, took an irrevocable turn. Her studies continued with underground classes, she escaped being deported to Nazi Germany as a slave laborer, and she started to work professionally as an illustrator. And she began writing, influenced by the Krakow cultural scene and in particular through meeting Czeslaw Milosz, twelve years her senior. By 1949 she had a collection of poems ready to publish but it didn't pass socialist censorship (they had Disinformation Governance Boards back then too). Which is odd, because she began as a cheerleader for socialism (young people can be forgiven for lacking knowledge of economics and history; what excuse older people have, I don't know).

When her first book came out in 1952—*That's Why We Are All Alive*—it was a different manuscript and contained poems praising Lenin and the idealism of socialist youth. These poems of so-called socialist realism she later renounced and declined to reprint. Although she kept her party membership until the mid-sixties, in the fifties she was already going off the Marxist reservation into dissident activities, an intellectual awakening into freedom that was reflected in her poetry. It became at the same time broader and deeper, able to express large concepts and questions in an ever more personal and relatable way. Once she found her true voice, it would not and could not be stilled.

The poem we're looking at here, "Possibilities," is classic Szymborska, most likely written sometime between the mid-seventies and mid-eighties, and first collected in the volume *People on the Bridge* (1986). The form it takes could not be simpler, a litany of sentences, each of which begins with "I prefer". The brilliance emerges with the things she says she prefers, with the order in which they are arranged, and with her technique for giving special emphasis to some. While superficially the poem appears to be as simple and casual and meandering as a shopping list, there is a loose kind of order to it, and a rhetorical rhythm.

The most obvious antecedent is the Sermon on the Mount from the Gospel of Matthew, with its litany of phrases beginning with "Blessed are." But there are many other literary examples that might have been known to and influenced the author, such as Christopher Smart's "Jubilate Agno," especially the part beginning with "For I will consider my Cat Jeoffrey" (surely the greatest cat poem ever written, but that's a subject for another day). Come to think of it, I wonder if she ever heard Tom T. Hall's biggest hit, "I Love," a charming litany from America's Top 40 in 1973?

Whatever the inspiration, the litany form allows her to explore some of her favorite themes, namely the worth of the individual and the meaning, if any, of human existence. Big subjects for such a humble-seeming bit of verse. The poet lists thirty-one things that she prefers—that is to say, that she not only likes, but likes more than the possible alternatives. This may be one source for the poem's title. Of the thirty-one things named, twenty-three fit onto one line. Eight of her preferences are enjambed onto a second line, setting them apart for emphasis. We'll get to those in a moment. First, though, let's examine the overall impact of her preferences.

They define her; or rather, they begin to define her, because obviously she could have written a different list, and even alludes to that possibility near the end of the poem—another source for her poem's title. One can read the litany as her half of a conversation she would like (or prefer?) to have with the reader: I prefer this; what do you prefer? And as readers we find ourselves engaging in that conversation almost unwittingly. "Oh, so you prefer cats, cat lady? Well, I prefer dogs," says the dog lady reader. She's wrong, of course, says the cat-loving essay writer, but that's the whole point of individuality. While our differences distinguish us, they don't have to divide us. Cat lovers and dog lovers can agree that animals are beautiful and to be appreciated and protected. We need not come to blows over the fact that one animal is an eternal infant that must be coddled and catered to every second of every day, whereas the other is an intelligent, independent feline.

She's telling us who she is here, and by implication asking us who we are. The third line of the poem, "I prefer the oaks along the Warta," refers to the Warta River, and thus locates her in Poland, if we didn't already know. What does that tell us? Well, in the last century the Poles have seen it all: conquered and raped by Nazis, conquered and raped by Soviets, decades of subjugation, the rise of a Polish Pope and Solidarity, the collapse of communism, and finally the ugly, messy, ambivalent but exhilarating experience of freedom, more or less. Is it any wonder so many of the best modern poets have been Polish? They know things, deep things, that most of the rest of us do not.

There are no overtly political or religious opinions given in the poem. And yet it is not hard to sift out a kind of personal credo for Szymborska in some of these lines:

> I prefer the earth in civvies.
> I prefer conquered to conquering countries . . .
> I prefer the hell of chaos to the hell of order.

When she says "I prefer Dickens to Dostoyevsky," is she expressing a general preference for humor over tragedy? And is that fair? After all, Raskolnikov is a pretty funny name. Or is it that her people suffered too much at the hands of the Russians for her to want to hear about the sufferings of Russians? I wish she were here so I could ask her. Meanwhile the simple declarative statements of this poem echo in the mind of the reader as questions. Very clever, these Poles!

Now let's look at the eight enjambed preferences that bleed over onto a second line, demanding special attention. The first comes early in the poem, lines five and six: "I prefer myself liking people / to myself loving mankind."

What a masterpiece of understatement! Mankind is an abstraction, easy to say you love it because it demands nothing of you. "People" are individuals, and merely liking them, a much more modest ambition than loving, requires that we know and accept their quirks and faults.

The second enjambed preference is this: "I prefer not to maintain / that reason is to blame for everything." That seems . . . reasonable. And maybe it's also an oblique way of saying that reason sometimes gets blamed for the crimes of unreason.

The third enjambment is probably the most famous: "I prefer the absurdity of writing poems / to the absurdity of not writing poems." Again, very clever, because she disarms us at the start by admitting that writing poems is absurd. Not to go all existential on you, but which human activities are not absurd? If we must choose between absurdities—and it appears we must—then I choose with Szymborska to write poems.

Her fourth run-on line is this: "I prefer, where love's concerned, nonspecific anniversaries / that can be celebrated every day." Yes! says every man who ever lived. But he had better say it to himself or there will be hell to pay. Her larger point, however, is a longing for less regimentation, a feeling that surfaces multiple times in "Possibilities."

"I prefer moralists / who promise me nothing." Thus runs her fifth enjambment. Meaning, I think, the moralist who promises something is either lying or deluded, the blind leading the blind. This recalls to me what Czeslaw Milosz wrote: "To be frank, hers is a very grim poetry."

Enjambed preference number six provides an escape hatch of sorts for author and reader if they don't happen to be satisfied with any of the statements in this poem: "I prefer many things that I haven't mentioned here / to many things I've also left unsaid." This sounds to me a little bit like the Ninth Amendment from the Bill of Rights, which reads, "The enumeration in the Constitution, of certain rights, shall not be construed to deny or disparage others retained by the people." One scholar referred to it as "the forgotten Ninth Amendment." Szymborska's similar caveat here reminds us that human beings, and the universe they inhabit, are full of contingencies. Everything could have very easily been different.

I admit to being somewhat mystified by her next-to-last enjambed preference: "I prefer zeroes on the loose / to those lined up behind a cipher." That's most evocative. I'm just not sure what's being evoked. It's worth mentioning that "cipher" means both "zero" and "code"—perhaps a little self-deprecating joke about needing to decode the poem, and that exercise adding up to zero? Anyway, maybe we don't need to know exactly what it means. This is poetry after all; some ambiguity comes with the territory. As Billy Collins says, "Most impressive is how Szymborska's poetry manages to be plainspoken and mysterious at the same time."

The eighth and final enjambment makes a most fitting end: "I prefer keeping in mind even the possibility / that existence has its own reason for being." Simultaneously these lines are a callback to the poem's title and to the mention of reason in the second enjambment. This imposes some form on what otherwise might appear to be a study in formlessness. As much as she dislikes being ordered about, she does enjoy subjecting her poems to order. But then she is a human being, and Wislawa Szymborska, which is to say, a creature of delightful and improbable contradictions.

Impossibilities

(after "Possibilities" by Wislawa Szymborska)

I believe in questions.
I believe in those who aren't so cocksure.
I believe strays make the best pets
and the best thoughts are stray thoughts.
I believe none of us is fashioned in the image of god
but perhaps cats are.
Like the Queen in *Alice in Wonderland* I've believed
as many as six impossible things before breakfast,
and even more when I've gone hungry.
I believe everything happens for a reason,
the details of which are carefully hidden from us.
It's easy to believe in beauty
because it's all around me all the time.

Equally easy to believe in ugliness
because I've looked within myself without blinking.
I believe in "Nothing that is not there and the nothing that is"
because Wallace Stevens is the god of poetry
and I worship him daily.
I do believe in nothing, its omnipresence, its palpability.
I believe in everything too—
after all, some part of it may turn out to be non-illusory.
If I believe anything, it's that
the Beatles and J. S. Bach and Bernard Herrmann
will live forever, and if forever isn't a thing
we'll have to invent a god to make it one.
I believe in silence, call it a faith
in something I've never actually heard.
I believe in baby turtles and tadpoles and love at first sight
and all hopeful beginnings.
Even more do I believe in
the splendors of autumn, breathtaking endings.
I believe unconditionally in those who read this,
somewhat less so in he who writes it,
though by some miracle of grace and mystery and luck
I believe he does have his moments
like the stopped clock that is right twice a day.

LUCILLE CLIFTON

the message of crazy horse

By Lucille Clifton

i would sit in the center of the world,
the Black Hills hooped around me and
dream of my dancing horse. my wife

was Black Shawl who gave me the daughter
i called They Are Afraid Of Her.
i was afraid of nothing

except Black Buffalo Woman.
my love for her i wore
instead of feathers. i did not dance

i dreamed. i am dreaming now
across the worlds. my medicine is strong.
my medicine is strong in the Black basket
of these fingers. i come again through this

Black Buffalo woman. hear me;
the hoop of the world is breaking.
fire burns in the four directions.
the dreamers are running away from the hills.
i have seen it. i am crazy horse.

FROM ONE AMERICAN ORIGINAL TO ANOTHER: LUCILLE CLIFTON ON CRAZY HORSE

If I ever manage to finish my first novel, some people are bound to ask, "Which parts are real, and which are fiction?" The answer will be, "It's all fiction, and it's all real." Meaning: I'm making it up, even the parts seemingly drawn from my own life, and if I do my job well, the story will reveal some novel (no pun intended) aspects of our shared reality, something new under the sun that only my imagination and life experience could bring about. Anyway, don't hold your breath.

"To know thyself is the beginning of wisdom," said Socrates; and, he might have added, the beginning of the writer's journey as well. But not the end. The whole point of the writer's awareness is surely to enter imaginatively into the hearts and minds of other characters and things, people, animals, plants, the world itself. This imagining usually starts with the first tool of human understanding, also the first tool in the poet's toolbox: analogy, or simile, likeness or its opposite, unlikeness.

Which brings us to Lucille Clifton (1936–2010). Being born a Black woman in America, and coming of age just as the civil rights movement was taking off, she wrote frequently and movingly about those experiences. A little younger than Maya Angelou (born 1928) and a little older than Nikki Giovanni (born 1943), she has much in common with those two contemporaries and other African American writers. What sets her apart from them and from almost any other poets of her generation is her unique combination of gifts, particularly her gift for empathy and her gift for concision. The former is what enables her to inhabit the spirit of Crazy Horse; the latter is largely responsible for making the result so memorable.

Clifton wrote five poems about the Lakota Oglala Sioux war chief who orchestrated the defeat of General Custer at the Battle of Little Bighorn in 1876. The poems "the death of crazy horse," "crazy horse names his daughter," "crazy horse instructs the young men but in their grief they forget," and "the message of crazy horse" all appear in the volume *Next* (1987). The fifth poem, "witko," appears in the final book of poetry Clifton published during her lifetime, *Voices* (2008).

We are looking today at "the message of crazy horse," the last of the four poems about him in *Next*. It serves as a comment on his life and the state of the world, made all these years later by his own spirit, as pictured by Clifton. The poem contains eighteen lines of free verse broken into five stanzas, the first three consisting of three lines each, the fourth of four lines and the fifth of five lines, a breakdown that suggests a homemade kind of form. One reason the poem works as well as it does is that Clifton's concise language matches the laconic nature of Native oratory. You feel that if she and Crazy Horse had ever met, each would have understood the other's refusal to waste words.

The first three stanzas, the shorter ones, recount the emotional and spiritual highlights of his life—which, significantly, do not include his battle triumphs. I take this pointed omission of the events for which he is most famous as a reminder that the necessities and duties of war were thrust upon him, not something he wished for or welcomed. In this, ironically, he has much more in common with an earlier American warrior, George Washington, than with his contemporary and opponent George Custer.

In the dramatic monologue that Clifton has crafted for him, the spirit of Crazy Horse begins at the beginning:

> i would sit in the center of the world,
> the Black Hills hooped around me and
> dream of my dancing horse [. . .]

Almost all people feel a special love for their homeland, and may also feel, or even believe, that it's the center of the world. The Lakota and other members of the Oglala Sioux band believed the Black Hills to be the literal center of the world—not just of their world—and anyone who has visited there might be tempted to agree with them. To paraphrase a line from later in the poem, their medicine is strong. So it is appropriate that "the message of crazy horse" mentions his Black Hills homeland first. What might seem odd is that he mentions his horse before his wife, daughter and lover. What's that about? I think it's because he was famed as a horseman and "horse" became part of his name before he fell in love, took a wife and fathered a child. He's simply telling his story chronologically. It may also be an oblique way of getting his war deeds into the poem after all, seeing as his skills as a rider were crucial to his war victories.

All he says in the poem about the woman Black Shawl is that she was his wife and bore him the daughter he named They Are Afraid of Her, though no one ever got the chance to be afraid of her as she died at age three. (There was a second wife later, Nellie Larrabee, daughter of a French trader and a Cheyenne woman, but she informed on Crazy Horse for the U.S. military, so the sincerity of that marriage is doubtful.) The poem starts to take off at the juncture between the end of stanza two and the beginning of stanza three:

i was afraid of nothing

except Black Buffalo Woman.
my love for her i wore
instead of feathers. [. . .]

Black Buffalo Woman was the love of his life. There were difficulties; they never married. Instead she wed a brave named No Water. However, the love between her and Crazy Horse continued to smolder, and one day they ran off together. When No Water caught up with them he shot Crazy Horse in the face with a pistol, leaving a permanent scar in the shape of a lightning bolt, which fit another part of the prophecy from his vision quest. You can't make this stuff up!

The line about not wearing feathers is another reference to Crazy Horse's life-changing vision, in which he was instructed not to wear war paint or a traditional feather headdress into battle. As long as he dressed modestly and didn't take scalps or other war trophies, he would be victorious and could not be killed in battle. For the most part, these prophecies proved to be true. The only time he was seriously wounded in combat was when he broke his vow by taking a scalp. More than a year after the Battle of Little Bighorn, when it was clear his cause was lost, Crazy Horse surrendered to the U.S. authorities and on September 5, 1877, wound up at Fort Robinson, Nebraska. That night he was bayoneted by a guard, supposedly while trying to escape, and died hours later. His parents collected the remains the next morning and laid him to rest in a location that remains secret to this day.

Back to the poem. This is about a poem, remember? After the three opening stanzas recounting highlights of Crazy Horse's time on earth, the narrative slips into high gear:

[. . .] i did not dance

i dreamed. i am dreaming now
across the worlds. my medicine is strong.
my medicine is strong in the Black basket
of these fingers. [. . .]

The last words of stanza three refer again to his vision quest, which told him he was not to engage in the usual war dances. As reimagined by Clifton, his mission both before and after death was dreaming. One of the author's chief poetic devices, just as it is one of the chief rhetorical devices of Native oratory, is reiteration. It's been sneaking up on us in stanzas one through three in the use of the word "Black"—capitalized because in each instance it is part of a proper name—and in the word "afraid"—first as part of his daughter's name, and then to describe the one thing he is afraid of, Black Buffalo Woman, thus neatly tying up the two reiterated words together.

The use of reiteration reaches its peak in stanza four, which can be considered the hinge of the poem, the place where it turns. "i dreamed", Crazy Horse says, and coming right after the life highlights of stanzas one through three, this tells us that his dream, his vision, was the key to his life. "i am dreaming now across the worlds", he continues, which tells us that his dream is also the key to his afterlife. Then comes the only reiteration of a complete phrase in the poem: "my medicine is strong. / my medicine is strong in the Black basket / of these fingers." Well, his medicine would have to be strong for his spirit to still be out there somewhere with something important to convey to us. And what an evocative, mysterious image that is, "the Black basket / of these fingers." I understand it as a reference to his physical death and the way the fingers of the Black Hills continue to hold his remains in an undisclosed location. Is that the reason "Black" is once again capitalized? Or is this the place where the author asserts her own personal identification with Crazy Horse, her Blackness linking her to this notable member of another oppressed and dispossessed group? Both, I think. And as Bob Dylan says somewhere (I believe in an early *Playboy* interview), "Mystery is a traditional fact."

Another mystery is the second mention of Black Buffalo Woman that begins the final stanza, number five. Special emphasis is being given to her, because her name is the only one mentioned twice in the poem, underscoring her centrality to the speaker. The most mysterious thing about it, to me, is that Clifton chooses not to capitalize the "w" in "woman" this time. I have no idea what this means though it is clearly deliberate. The only other name in which the initial letters are not capitalized is that of Crazy Horse himself, in both the title of the poem and the last line (and also in the use of a lower-case "i" when he speaks in the first person). This is not mysterious. Rather, it reflects the man's essential humility, something he shares with the author who uses a lower-case "i" in her other poems after the manner of e. e. cummings.

After invoking Black Buffalo Woman's name again and asking her to hear him, Crazy Horse delivers his new vision, and unlike his original vision quest it is not a happy or hopeful one:

> the hoop of the world is breaking.
> fire burns in the four directions.
> the dreamers are running away from the hills.
> i have seen it. i am crazy horse.

Only here, in the climax to this remarkable poem, does it become plain that we are reading an apocalyptic vision. The line "the hoop of the world is breaking" reminds us of a similar line near the beginning of the vision vouchsafed to W. B. Yeats in "The Second Coming": "Things fall apart; the centre cannot hold". Knowing that Clifton was quite familiar with the King James Bible, I also hear an echo of the apocalypse from Revelation 1:18: "I am he that liveth, and was dead; and behold, I am alive for evermore, Amen, and have the keys of hell and of death." This sounds very like her Crazy Horse, yes? And the fire burning in the next line resonates with those of us raised in a Christian culture to fear Hell.

Yet the worst news is saved for the penultimate line, "the dreamers are running away from the hills". It was bad enough that the U.S. government forcibly removed the Natives from their homes and homeland. This line brings us right up to the present, in which the dreamers, the visionaries, have fled from what gives them visions without being forced. To quote the Bible a final time, "Where there is no vision, the people perish" (Proverbs

29:18). With this line, I believe, the poem comes full circle, making its own hoop. The identification of author Lucille Clifton with the speaker of her dramatic monologue, Crazy Horse, becomes complete. She too is a visionary. Without the visions of dreamers like her and Crazy Horse, the people indeed perish, and perhaps also the earth on which they walk.

The last line—"i have seen it. i am crazy horse."—serves as a signature and a bona fide. This is the same Crazy Horse whose original vision proved to be true. We can trust him on this one. And the power of the vision comes as much from understatement as anything, the understatement common to Native oratory and Clifton's brilliant poetics.

Near Death

Flying into Phoenix on a Friday morning
we hit a wind shear so sharp
it knocked us sideways and down,
dropping 5,000 feet in a minute and a half,
the longest ninety seconds of our lives.
Every person on that plane
knew they were about to perish in it.
Suddenly weightless, we levitated out of our seats
and headfirst into the cabin ceiling,
meals and drinks sailing, luggage bursting
from the overhead bins into skulls and bodies
already reeling. Even the flight attendants
were screaming, and the young woman next to me
dug her nails into my arm and shrieked,
"We're crashing! We're crashing!"
Ever the gentleman, and always helpful in a crisis,
I reminded her of what Crazy Horse said
right before the Battle of the Little Big Horn:

"Today is a good day to die."
"What the fuck are you talking about?"
she yelled, but it worked—for a few
crucial seconds she was distracted from her fear.
I was afraid too, of course, though oddly
not for my life or death,
and after we had landed safely, I realized why.
Being hit and run and left for dead
by a semi-truck driver some years ago
had made me painfully aware that I was not
ready for death, that my soul
and psyche were in terrible shape.
Since then I had slain what inner demons I could
and put the rest in chains. At last I was living
as authentically as I knew how.
I had done the most terrifying thing imaginable—
become a father. I had even dared to start writing.
I had everything to live for and no wish to die.
This everyday American mongrel,
part Finnish, part Irish, part German Jew,
2.6 percent Neanderthal
and one sixty-fourth Shawnee
from the mighty war chief Corn Stalk,
this mostly white man is not worthy
to share the same sentence with Crazy Horse.
Yet by virtue of our common humanity
I claimed and still claim the right
to find inspiration in his final recorded words:
"Today is a good day to die."
And also to live, great spirit,
and also to live.

GABRIELA MISTRAL

Slow Rain *[first version]*

By Gabriela Mistral

translated by H. R. Hays

This timorous, sorrowful water,
Like a child that suffers,
Before it touches the earth,
    Falls fainting.

The tree and the wind are quiet
And in the stupendous silence,
These clear and bitter tears
    Keep falling.

The sky is like an immense heart
Which opens bitterly.
It does not rain; it is bleeding, slowly
    Abundantly.

Men indoors at the hearthstone
Feel none of this bitterness,
This gift of sorrowful water
    From above us.

This wide and weary descent
Of conquered waters
Toward the earth, reclining
    And exhausted.

The lifeless water is falling
As quietly as in a dream,
Like the slight creations
　　Dreams are full of.

It rains . . . and like a tragic jackal
Night lies in wait in the mountains.
Out of the earth, in darkness,
　　What will rise up?

And shall you sleep while, outside,
This sickly lifeless water of death
　　Is falling?

The Mystery of Gabriela Mistral

Actually, there are several mysteries surrounding Gabriela Mistral. Which is odd, given that she was the first Latin American author and one of the first women to receive a Nobel Prize in Literature (1945). Her work is known and loved throughout the Spanish-speaking world, particularly in her own country, Chile. Yet she remains very little heard of in English. In our current age you would think doctoral candidates would be falling over themselves to write dissertations on this groundbreaking Hispanic woman writer who was almost certainly a lesbian (though she was so secretive about her emotional life that some slight mystery still lingers over that question).

The outward facts of her life are well established. She was born Lucila Godoy Alcayaga in Vicuña, Chile, on April 7, 1889, and died in Hempstead, New York, on January 10, 1957, at the age of sixty-seven. Her father abandoned the family when she was two years old, inflicting the first of several significant wounds by a man in her life. In 1906 she fell in love with a railroad worker, Romelio Ureta, who committed suicide for unrelated reasons in 1909. The next man she loved married another woman and broke Lucila's heart. She was deeply hurt, but strong. She had been supporting herself and her mother since the age of fifteen, working as a teacher's aide in Compañía Baja, a coastal town. By 1904 she was already writing and publishing poems in local newspapers under various pseudonyms, beginning a lifelong habit of guarding her privacy. Ten years later, in 1914, she won a national literary competition with her *Sonnets on Death* (*Sonetas de la muerta*). These poems responded to the death of her first lover, the death of love itself, and perhaps also the death of her father, who passed away in 1911 still estranged from his family.

The literary prize was a turning point. From that time on, with few exceptions, she adopted the pen name by which she is still known. Depending on which version of the story you prefer to believe, she took "Gabriela" either from Italian writer Gabriele D'Annunzio or the angel Gabriel, and she took "Mistral" either from Nobel-winning French poet Frédéric Mistral or the mistral wind so common in Provence. The pseudonym was at least partly motivated by fear of losing her job if her employers became aware of her unusually frank and disturbing poems. Her fame as an educator was growing as rapidly as her literary renown. Teaching jobs in country and coastal towns gave way to a position in the Department of Education in the capital, Santiago. This led to her being headhunted by the Mexican Minister of Education to help reform his country's system of education in 1922. She was only thirty-three. Extraordinary!

Meanwhile she continued to publish poems, prose poems, fables, stories and essays on a multitude of topics, including the rights of women and children. Though she clearly needed to express herself and wanted her work to be known, she seemed curiously indifferent to putting out a book, another mysterious lifetime quirk. And in fact her first book was not her idea and wasn't even published in her own country originally. *Desolacion* (1922) came about because a Professor of Spanish Literature at New York's Columbia University, Federico de Onis, had taught her poetry to his students. Her work bowled them over, and when they learned she had no book as of yet, they assembled one themselves and published it through the university's imprint.

Mistral would deserve a place in the history of literature if only for her friendship with and her encouraging and mentoring of the young Pablo Neruda, fifteen years her junior. The parallels between their careers are worth recounting. Not only do they share the honor of having received a Nobel Prize. Each of them won that prize for a body of work that included poems written when they were mere teenagers, poems that made them instantly famous. Neruda and Mistral shared a preference for writing under a pseudonym. They also shared a devotion to social justice, pursued by Neruda through the communist party politics of his day, and by Mistral through her more independent path, which, it is fair to say, did more actual good. Finally, they shared in benefitting from Chile's enlightened policy of letting its writers and artists serve in a consular capacity throughout the world. (Would that the United States were half as civilized!)

The poem we're looking at here, "La Lluvia Lenta" ("Slow Rain"), was written in 1914 when the poet was twenty-five and became part of her first book, *Desolacion*, in the section called "Naturaleza" ("Nature"). The first English translation was by H. R. Hays. It appeared in *Poetry* magazine in May 1943 in an issue devoted to Latin American poets. That same year Hays, one of the finest translators of Hispanic poetry, assembled an anthology called *12 Spanish American Poets*, which did much to bring the best writers of the region to the awareness of North Americans. Early translations of Borges, Guillen, Vallejo and Mistral's own student Neruda are there—but not Mistral herself. In fact there are no women poets at all! To me this is a shocking omission, especially given that Hays knew her work and admired it enough to translate it for *Poetry*. Chalk up another Mistral mystery.

In the original Spanish, the poem consists of eight stanzas. Each stanza begins with three octosyllabic lines and ends with a tetrasyllabic line (i.e., four syllables, half as many). When I say the lines have eight syllables and four syllables, I am counting not the grammatical syllables, which are sometimes more or less than that, but the poetical syllables, the stressed ones. Does that make sense? Anyway, that's how they do prosody in Latin America, so the experts tell me. The second and fourth lines rhyme. Spanish being a much more rhyme-rich language than English, it is no doubt wise of Hays not to attempt a rhyming translation. Most of the rhyming translations that I've seen of Mistral's work in old anthologies are stilted and convey little of the music of the originals.

Hays manages to bring quite a lot of that music into English, using assonance and alliteration and a few other devices while keeping the structure. The first stanza establishes the direction and tone:

> This timorous, sorrowful water,
> Like a child that suffers,
> Before it touches the earth,
> > Falls fainting.

Water in general, as both symbol and fact, is a life-bringer. In a rural farming community like the one Mistral grew up in, it is everything. Without rain there will be drought, crops will fail, children will go hungry and farmers will sink even farther into poverty. Why isn't she celebrating the rain?

Perhaps because water is also a feminine symbol, and at this time in her life she quite rightly felt hindered, harassed and oppressed as a woman with a significant literary gift and a passion for teaching children who was banging her head against various walls. I don't know whether this poem was written before she won the national poetry prize that brought her first fame (both events occurred in 1914). But almost all of her triumphs were ahead of her, yet unknown. Among other things, the Catholic Church had denied her entrance into one of its teacher training schools because of her unorthodox writings, and she had to study for her teaching certificate on her own. This and similar happenings may partly explain the unrelenting sense of sadness and defeat in this poem.

Stanza two speaks of the "stupendous silence" in which "These clear and bitter tears / Keep falling." The well-worn trope of tears-as-rain gains power from the poem's (actually the translator's) first use of internal rhyme with "clear" and "tears". And now we can see that the poem is an extreme example of the pathetic fallacy, a projection of Mistral's deep suffering and grief onto the natural world. Stanza three makes it even more personal and painful, calling the sky "an immense heart / Which opens bitterly. / It does not rain: it is bleeding [. . .]" That is quite an imaginative leap, from rain to tears to blood, in such a short space. Women are fated to bleed every month, a blessing or a curse depending on who's doing the defining. Yet just as with the rain, the future of the human race utterly depends upon this difficult flow.

Just in case we missed the explicitly feminine aspect of this imagery, these metaphors, stanza four offers a stark contrast with another leading gender:

> Men indoors at the hearthstone
> Feel none of this bitterness,
> This gift of sorrowful water
>   From above us.

Stanza four is notable for several reasons. It cleverly, one might almost say satirically, identifies men, not women, as the real homebodies who hide indoors from the troubles of the world. Why do they not feel the bitterness of this slow rain? Because it is not woven into their very being as it is with women, who are part of nature, one with nature, in ways that men can never be (of course there are ways in which the opposite is also true, but they are not the focus of this poem). This stanza further affirms that the rain, while still sorrowful, is also a gift. What's more, a gift from "above us," i.e., god or the gods.

In stanza five we hear of "conquered waters" whose descent toward the earth is "wide and weary". The earth is described as "reclining / And exhausted." Rather late in the game, stanza six introduces the idea that the slow rain may be a dream:

> The lifeless water is falling
> As quietly as in a dream,
> Like the slight creations
>   Dreams are full of.

That's interesting. Does this suggestion of dreaming undercut what has come before or strengthen it? I think it does the latter. As we know, the seemingly "slight creations" of dreams often hold tremendous significance. At this time in her life, before she returned to the Catholic Church, Mistral was searching, questioning, and found an affinity for theosophy and Buddhism. This was also the period when she was most influenced by the modernist poets of Latin America, with their deep, complex symbology of images. The founder of *modernismo*, Rubén Darío of Nicaragua, was one of the early champions of Mistral's work before his death in 1916.

By far the most interesting thing about stanza six, however, is that Mistral later cut it from the poem. I have no idea why. In my opinion that edit was a mistake, but of course it's her poem, and anyone is free to read it both ways and decide for themselves, just as we can with the dueling versions of W. H. Auden's "In Memory of W. B. Yeats."

Stanza seven introduces another sharp turn in the narrative:

> [. . .] and like a tragic jackal
> Night lies in wait in the mountains.
> Out of the earth, in darkness,
>   What will rise up?

What indeed? Whatever it may be, it merits the second use of an internal rhyme by the translator, "tragic jackal". In this case, however, the rhyme does exist in the original. The implication of the imagery is vaguely but disturbingly ominous. Coming after the rest of the poem, I take it to refer to the thwarted gifts of womanhood, which, when deflected by a world run by men, do not lead to a happy conclusion.

The final stanza, number eight in the early uncut version of the poem we're looking at, continues the unwholesome water imagery: "And shall you sleep while, outside, / This sickly lifeless water of death / Is falling?" Undoubtedly, I feel, the poet asks this question of herself. The ending is thus a call for her to wake up. While it's impossible to get too specific an interpretation of all this morbid imagery, it's fair to take the final stanza as a call to action. The translator does his part to emphasize the conclusion by making this stanza only three lines in English, though it is four in the original Spanish. The poet, the dreamer of dreams, is the one challenging herself to make those dreams a reality. She knows she must be a conscious dreamer, one to heed both the call to creative vision and the call to train the minds of children, the two calls she pursued faithfully all her life.

Wasted Years

I loved and hated a woman, but mostly loved.
She loved and hated me, but mostly hated.
When hope is gone its cousin, hopelessness, remains,
the ugly familiarity of which can be a kind of comfort.
I held a succession of meaningless jobs
made even more poignant because they enabled me
to pay for the privilege of being hated.
Clearly, I was not in my right mind.
The years crawled by like crippled dogs
trying to cross a major highway.
I couldn't write anything serious
as that would've killed me instantly.
Instead I wrote humor with heartbreak always
just beneath the surface, humor as a form of despair.
To make the time pass I read thousands of books,
which was like shooting myself in the head
with a nail gun firing the truths of others.
And then came the only good part
of every nightmare, the part where I wake up.

H. D.

Evening

By H. D.

The light passes
from ridge to ridge,
from flower to flower—
the hepaticas, wide-spread
under the light
grow faint—
the petals reach inward,
the blue tips bend
toward the bluer heart
and the flowers are lost.

The cornel-buds are still white,
but shadows dart
from the cornel-roots—
black creeps from root to root,
each leaf
cuts another leaf on the grass,
shadow seeks shadow,
then both leaf
and leaf-shadow are lost.

THE EVER-CHANGING IMAGES OF H. D.

Hilda Doolittle (1886–1961), forever known by the pen name that Ezra Pound suggested to her, H. D., has seen her literary reputation rise swiftly, fall slowly during her life, and then even more slowly rise again since her death, thanks to a reappraisal that is still ongoing. Quite a few readers, myself included, hold her work to be on a par with that of Pound, Eliot, Williams, Stevens, or any of the other male writers who ushered in the twentieth-century revolution in English-speaking poetry. Sadly, this was never the general opinion while she was alive, not even at the height of her early fame. Nor can the reassessment of her career be considered complete as long as she has no volume of *Complete* or *Collected Poems* (the *Collected Poems* that is in print only includes work from 1912 to 1944, before her important later poems were published).

The explanation for this lies first in how her career was launched and who launched it. As with almost everything involving American literature in the early twentieth century, the answer is Ezra Pound. Name a literary fad, movement or controversy from that period, and Ezra Pound will be at the center of it, making things happen, for better or worse. He boosted the careers of countless writers he barely knew or didn't care about personally, but with Ezra and Hilda it was always personal. They had been friends and lovers as young people when they both lived in Pennsylvania. His first serious poems were inspired by her, and vice versa. When he moved to Europe in search of a more hospitable place to put down artistic roots, she followed soon after. Though their on-again, off-again romance faltered, they remained friends and shared creative ideals. And when she began producing outstanding poems, he wanted them to be seen and appreciated.

Like James Dickey and L. E. Sissman (remember him? You should), Pound could have made a living as an advertising copywriter if he had the stomach for it. He had a genius for promotional phrase-making. He understood that inventing schools of literature would help the mass of readers understand that something new was afoot. To beat the drums for Hilda he concocted the notion of Imagism, and declared her the leading exemplar, along with Richard Aldington and Amy Lowell. It worked. Almost too well. Pound sent three of H. D.'s poems to Harriet Monroe, who dutifully published them in *Poetry*. The magazine was to remain one of H. D.'s most loyal supporters from that point on.

It's worth quoting Pound's original Imagist manifesto in full, as it offers sound advice not only for Imagists but for any poet trying to do a good job:

> We were agreed on the three principles following:
>
> 1. Direct treatment of the "thing" whether subjective or objective.
> 2. To use absolutely no word that does not contribute to the presentation.
> 3. As regarding rhythm, to compose poetry in the sequence of the musical phrase, not in the sequence of a metronome.

There would be other manifestos, all of them longer and more belabored. This first one is actually the most imagistic: concise and clear. However, as with all movements, there were soon splinterings and dilutions. Barely a year after announcing Imagism, Pound unveiled the much goofier and more nebulous Vorticism and declared that H. D. was really one of those (don't ask me to define it, as it's complicated and boring). Imagism limped on for more than a decade, co-opted by Amy Lowell and others less talented than H. D. Pound, ever the literary comedian when he wasn't playing Mussolini's court jester on the radio, took to calling the movement he had started "Amygism."

But to return to our subject, which, after all, is H. D. We cannot let Pound dominate this essay merely because he dominated her early life and career and quite generously got her started. After her early Imagism phase, which did result in some of the greatest poems written in the last century—including the one everybody knows, "Oread," and the lesser-known one we'll be looking at here, "Evening"—she kept developing as an artist, which is what every artist does if she really is an artist.

Once out of Pound's orbit she became a rogue planet whirling through the alien spaces of bohemian Europe. Her personal life can only be described as a complex mess, though probably a necessary mess because, as a bisexual woman pulled equally in two directions, she could not seem to find permanent fulfillment in a monogamous relationship with a person of any sex. Her happiest home life appears to have been when she was part of two longstanding menages. The love of her life was with the English novelist Bryher (Annie Winifred Ellerman). Yes, they had mononyms back then too. Suck it Madonna, Sia and Rihanna! She married her fellow Imagist Richard Aldington, and stayed married for two decades even when the relationship died after a couple of years.

H. D. had long accepted her bifurcated desires but wished to understand them better, and how they affected her art. It was this that impelled her to undergo psychoanalysis, first with the Freudian Hanns Sachs in 1928, and then with Sigmund Freud himself in 1933–34. She felt tremendously helped by this experience, as a person and as an artist, and later wrote several accounts of it that were collected into the book *Tribute to Freud* (1956). She believed that this psychological work was in part what enabled her to embark on the ambitious new style that informed her later poetry: still imagistic, still inspired by the ancient Greeks, but now encompassing larger themes of civilization, history, war, spirituality, and the role of the feminine psyche.

In a way, these mature works were similar in scope to Pound's *Cantos*, except that is not fair to either author, despite their mutual lifelong influence. Pound quite correctly referred to his *Cantos* as "a botched masterpiece," whereas H. D.'s later works hold up much better. To put it bluntly, he lost his sanity, she found hers. Of particular note are the three volumes of verse she produced during World War II, *The Walls Do Not Fall* (1944), *Tribute to the Angels* (1945) and *The Flowering of the Rod* (1946). The first of these contains a brave and harrowing firsthand account of the London Blitz, arguably the finest poetry to come out of the war.

I wish there was room in an essay of this size to examine these and other later books and book-length poems by H. D. Unfortunately, there is not. So we shall content ourselves by examining one of her early poems in the Imagiste style that made her famous. At least this one, "Evening," from her first full-length collection *Sea Garden* (1916), has not been over-anthologized or over-analyzed.

The poem consists of two free verse stanzas, the first of ten lines, the second of nine lines. The lines themselves are short, ranging from two words to six words, roughly the length of a breath. As the title suggests, the poet is describing the coming of the night. Taken simply on that level, it is a work of stunning, if quiet, beauty.

It is so clear, so immediate in its perceptions that it is hard to believe it was written more than a century ago. Most of the nature poetry being written then was pure drivel, having little to do with actual observations of the natural world. Usually it was a lot of sentimental, romantic or religious notions attached to a few vague images and rhyming with all the subtlety of a cuckoo clock. Mercifully, drivel seldom survives, yet there is a favorite form of drivel in every age, and most of the readers living through an age love it, just as most of them love the huge amount of drivel being written today. This is neither the time nor place to discuss what form drivel takes in our own age. Just know that a hundred years from now it will look really asinine, and if you were still alive then you would never stop apologizing for having anything to do with it.

Back to the poem!

The poem starts with light and ends in shadow. The first stanza moves quickly from larger, farther particulars to smaller, closer ones:

> The light passes
> from ridge to ridge,
> from flower to flower—
> the hepaticas, wide-spread
> under the light
> grow faint—

Note the reiterations of "ridge" and "flower" in lines two and three, which also constitute instances of internal rhymes and alliteration. Did you know the hepatica is a bisexual flower? I didn't either, until I looked it up. Its appearance here in a powerful early poem by the very out H. D. cannot be accidental. No sooner does she name the flowers than she notes in one of the poem's two shortest lines (for emphasis) that they "grow faint." One could also say, they begin to lose their distinctiveness, their individuality, their identity. What evening does to flowers, time, age and death do to us and all living things. And so here the other possible readings of the poem, aside from the sharp imagery, open up, just as, at the end of the first stanza:

the petals reach inward,
the blue tips bend
toward the bluer heart
and the flowers are lost.

Again, some nice alliteration with "blue," "bend" and "bluer." In what sense, though, are the flowers lost? To the eye of the poet, of course. Also to themselves? To the world? Once more we are invited to contemplate wider meanings of this daily transition. The action verbs "reach" and "bend" imply an agency that the flowers surely do not possess. And yet these verbs help put across the other meanings, and it is fair to ascribe some form of consciousness to plants, these mysterious things that respond so readily to sunlight, rain and even music.

If stanza one is about the dying of the light, stanza two is about the growth of evening's shadows. Or in a wider sense, the approach of death, sleep, oblivion. Once again a flower is involved. Significantly, however, it is not as specific as the hepaticas of stanza one. H. D. refers only to "cornel-buds" and "cornel-roots," which would make the plant some kind of dogwood. While the buds may be "still white," many dogwoods have yellow flowers. Calling them buds means they haven't bloomed yet, they aren't even open enough to be closed by the coming of evening:

[. . .] shadows dart
from the cornel-roots—
black creeps from root to root,
each leaf
cuts another leaf on the grass,
shadow seeks shadow,
then both leaf
and leaf-shadow are lost.

Note the parallel construction to stanza one, with action verbs now given to shadows instead of to flowers, and twice as many of them—"dart," "creeps," "cuts," "seeks." Once more there's abundant reiteration, alliteration and internal rhyming, with variations on "shadow," "root" and "leaf." Stanza two also ends with the word "lost." By this time, though, the loss has become complete. Evening, night, shadow has conquered all.

The more I study and meditate on this exquisitely brief and masterfully crafted poem, the better I like it. It remains a shining (or shadowy?) example of the poet's early style, a style that deservedly took the literary world by storm. If you enjoy it as much as I do, I urge you also to study her later work, which has all of the same qualities and more besides. H. D. never stopped growing, changing, and evolving as an artist. We could not wish for a better example to follow and honor, each of us in our own way.

Not Quite Awake

The house is still, almost,
a ticking clock,
the whisper of early morning traffic
on distant streets,
two crows arguing
about something in the meadow.
The sky overcast,
hiding the sunrise.
If the world has to end now
it will go quietly, like a convict
who has accepted his guilt.
Perhaps it already has
and I am standing attentively
in an imperceptible paradise.

JORGE LUIS BORGES

A Minor Poet

By Jorge Luis Borges

translated by Alastair Reid

The goal is oblivion.
I have arrived early.

AH, DID YOU ONCE SEE BORGES PLAIN?

Jorge Luis Borges needs no introduction, I think to myself. Then I think again, recalling that we are living through a new dark age when much of the past, including the literary past, is being discarded wholesale in a kind of cultural amnesia or cultural lobotomy. And I think perhaps I had better introduce him anyway.

He was born in 1899 in Buenos Aires, Argentina, and died in Geneva, Switzerland, in 1986 at the age of eighty-six. Among other things we can say about the young Borges, he would have instantly recognized the reference to a line by Browning in the title of this essay. He was raised to be bilingual, speaking only English until age four. His knowledge of English and American literature was encyclopedic, surpassing any other Latin American writer of his generation. No doubt this was instrumental in his eventual choice of profession: librarian. Has anyone ever written so often or so imaginatively of libraries and librarians?

Borges started writing as a child and never stopped, perhaps influenced by his father, Jorge Guillermo Borges Haslam, a successful lawyer and teacher, but a failed writer. As the son would later experience, the father also had deteriorating eyesight, and moved the family to Geneva, Switzerland, in 1914 so he could receive medical treatment. They remained abroad until 1921, after spending a few years in Spain. It was there that Borges affiliated briefly with the avant-garde Ultraist movement, which was a reaction against Modernismo.

Back in Buenos Aires, he wrote furiously, publishing his first book of poetry in 1923, *Fervor de Buenos Aires* (*Fervor of Buenos Aires*), and his second in 1925, *Luna de enfrente* (usually translated as *Moon Across the Way*, though in person I heard him call it *The Moon Across the Street*). In 1925 there also came his first book of essays, *Inquisiciones*, (*Inquiries*). He made important longtime friends, such as Victoria Ocampo, founder of *Sur* magazine, the country's leading literary organ, and Adolfo Bioy Casares, who would become his close collaborator. Although poetry was his first love, and he never gave it up, he devoted more time to the short prose hybrid forms on which much of his fame is justly based. Borges is almost certainly the most influential fiction writer who never completed a novel. He inspired not only generations of writers in his own language, but also in English and many others.

The other significant thing that happened during those early years was the gradual onset of his blindness. In 1928 he had the first of eight eye operations. Within twenty-five years he was completely blind. This tragedy affected every aspect of his existence. Yet he managed to find some blessings in it. One of his later books of poetry is called *Elogio de la sombra* (1969) (*In Praise of Darkness*). Of necessity, blindness sharpened his hearing and his memory, two gifts that made him a better poet.

Before I embark on an analysis of his tiny poem "A Minor Poet," I need to recount two of my own memories. The first is of a visit Borges made to Northwestern University in Chicago. I think it was 1974. He had been famous in America for two decades by that time. The place was packed. Borges spoke for a bit about his love for English and American literature, and how that love influenced his own work. He recited some favorite poems from memory, along with a few of his own. Then he took questions.

Someone who knew his work well asked what a particular line in one of the poems from his second book was about. I wish I could remember which line and which poem! Anyway, that's when he referred to the book as *The Moon Across the Street*. He was somewhat dismissive of his early work. "Honestly, I don't know what I meant," he admitted. "Probably I was just trying to come up with the most startling image possible. That's what I did in those days."

Another person asked who were his favorite American poets. Not surprisingly, he mentioned Whitman and Dickinson and Frost. But there was an audible gasp of surprise and embarrassment when he said he loved Carl Sandburg, then very much out of favor with the literati. Maybe he still is, I don't know. Borges quoted "Fog," the one we were all taught as schoolchildren, and I believe he mentioned "Chicago" and "Washington Monument by Night," two more great American poems, no matter what trivial fads and shunnings may occur in our little literary pond. Sandburg's love for his native city must have resonated with the man who had a lifelong love affair with his own Buenos Aires.

I asked a question as well, which is the subject of one of my two tribute poems accompanying this essay, the one called "What Borges Said" (the other is called "Another Minor Poet"). It was an idiotic question—what did he think of the horror and science fiction author H. P. Lovecraft? Still, he answered it in a way that made me feel slightly less idiotic while casually revealing the depth of his knowledge. How many American poets alive then could have done that? Precious few.

My question was perhaps the second stupidest one that day. I am pleased to report that the most imbecilic question was asked by another preening windbag. This nitwit wanted to know if Borges would comment on Thomas Pynchon's *Gravity's Rainbow* and what he called "the gravity of comedy." That sprawling novel had just been published the year before. Today many critics regard it as one of the finest American novels. That's as may be. Yet how fatuous to assume that Borges would have had any chance to read it. I doubt very much whether there was an audio or Braille version at that time. The only way Borges could have known the book is if he had had someone read it aloud to him, all 760 densely-packed, surreal and paranoid pages.

After the event, I had a chance to say hello and thank you to Borges. Just that, not even my name. But that was enough.

Fast-forward thirty-eight years to 2012. Life, divorce and the vagaries of my so-called career had exiled me to Lewiston, Idaho, away from my children and any trace of human civilization. It was the worst two years of my life. Except, there was a good university nearby in Moscow, Idaho, and also a top-notch independent bookstore, BookPeople. One night they had a special event featuring Willis Barnstone, an excellent poet and easily one of the two or three best translators in the English language. Right now I'm looking at a copy of his first published work, *80 Poems of Antonio Machado*, from 1959. Good luck finding that anywhere at any price, though I will gladly let you come to my house and read it while I sit nearby with a loaded revolver.

I said hello to Barnstone and thanked him for his many translations, singling out those he had done of Borges. That got him reminiscing and talking. We spent the next hour on a couch discussing Borges in general and that visit to Northwestern University in particular. It turned out Barnstone had been one of his assistants and handlers on that lecture tour. I had already met him, in fact, all those years ago. He was forty-seven on that day in 1974 and eighty-five as we sat in BookPeople chatting about it, and it was as if not a moment had passed. He remembered every detail of the talk by Borges and also the questions, including mine and the one from the fan of *Gravity's Rainbow*.

Meanwhile, I was shamelessly monopolizing him, and the other attendees were getting increasingly annoyed and restless. I reluctantly released Barnstone back into the wild, deeply moved by this unexpected encounter. Something had been reawakened in me: the love of poetry. Not just reading it, but trying to write it again. A couple of years later I abandoned humor writing after several decades with the *Onion* and stints writing for television and radio. I returned to my first love, poetry. And in part I have to thank Jorge Luis Borges and Willis Barnstone for realigning my chakras, or whatever that was on those two mysteriously connected occasions.

As you can see, this essay is very personal for me. They say you should never meet your heroes. However, I met one of mine in 1974—two, actually—and they did not disappoint.

The Borges poem we'll be looking at here is one of his shortest, only two lines and eight words (nine in the original Spanish), or eleven words counting the title, "A Minor Poet." It should not be confused with an earlier poem bearing a similar title and theme, "To a Minor Poet of the Greek Anthology," which has been beautifully rendered in English by W. S. Merwin. This later, much more concise poem was first included in the book *The Gold of the Tigers: Selected Later Poems* (1977), translated by Alastair Reid. Technically, it is part of a set of otherwise unrelated brief poems gathered under the title "Fifteen Coins." I believe this means we are allowed to quote it in full here, as it was originally part of another longer poem.

Regardless of how it was first presented to the world, it stands on its own:

A Minor Poet

The goal is oblivion.
I have arrived early.

In case you were wondering, it is just as simple and unadorned in the original Spanish as it is in English. It does not rhyme. It is too short to establish any other distinctive sound patterns involving alliteration or assonance. Nor does it feature any "startling images" like those that festooned his earliest poems, the ones I heard him speak of almost with contempt or regret. It was said that later he bought up any copies he could find of some of them, simply so that he could destroy them and return them to oblivion.

No, this little poem depends almost entirely upon the most direct, straightforward kind of statement. Yet so much is contained in it, I feel. The key word, I believe, is "goal." "The goal is oblivion." Not, "The result is oblivion," or "The thing that happens is oblivion," or "The destination is oblivion." The *goal*. Whose goal, though? Surely not the poet's. God's goal, maybe? The goal of the universe, or existence? How strange, if the goal of existence is nonexistence, as if existence is some sort of aberration. And why oblivion instead of, say, death or darkness or silence? Oblivion, total erasure, seems more final than any of those I suppose. These unspoken and unanswered questions linger in the mind long after reading the poem.

The second and last line—what would be the punchline if this were a joke (and perhaps it is in a way)—is a real heartbreaker: "I have arrived early." Of course, part of being a minor poet, the fate of nearly all of us, is that we never arrived anywhere at all. We tried, we gave it our best shot, we may even have written a few lines or a few poems worth remembering. Only they will not be remembered. Nor will we. Oh, oblivion, yes, there's a goal we all can meet! Some sooner than others, that's all.

We can think of this poem almost as one of those tantalizing fragments by Sappho (Willis Barnstone translated her too, check it out), pieces of lost poems so intense that even in partial form they remain poems in their own right. It's nearly a fractal of the earlier, longer poem (which is also a great poem), and yet it contains all that matters from that poem. It has not quite reached the goal of oblivion, though it is getting awfully close. Ironically, by writing it along with so many other memorable verses, Borges will not be arriving early at oblivion. Make no mistake, however, he will arrive at the place that receives us all, minor poets and major alike. And there may be worse things than oblivion. You could be the poor hapless fool who asked that silly question about *Gravity's Rainbow*. To quote yet another minor poet, "So long lives this, and this gives life to thee."

Another Minor Poet

(after "A Minor Poet" by Jorge Luis Borges)

The song I hope to sing is one
where the words march into the whiteness of the page
like Captain Robert Falcon Scott trudging toward the South Pole,
fated to arrive five weeks after Amundsen,
that damned Norwegian upstart, and even worse,
doomed to die on the return journey,
braving the vast Antarctic icebox again at forty below.

There is no shame in being the second man
to reach the Pole or walk on the Moon (who was that again?),
no dishonor in being the first forgotten,
snow-blind, descending into darkness by means of the light.
The sweet amnesia of snow and cold is no less merciful
than that of the poem never written, never published,
or perhaps, published and quickly lost among so many others.
Though we appear to be hurtling away from each other
we are all on the same journey,
unknowingly following imaginary, invisible longitudinal lines
that must meet in the long night at the wrong end of Earth.

What Borges Said

Argentina's greatest export, the maker
of fables disguised as essays
and poems disguised as translations,
was on a lecture tour
of the United States, already blind,
led around by Willis Barnstone
and other good friends.
I saw him at Northwestern University
but he never saw me,
and when my turn came
to ask him a question
all reason left me and I blurted out,
"What do you think of H. P. Lovecraft?"
He smiled and said,
"Wonderful imagination.
Terrible writer. But when a man
has a name like Lovecraft
he has already given us everything.
We need ask nothing more of him."

FEDERICO GARCIA LORCA

Home from a Walk

By Federico Garcia Lorca

translated by Robert Bly

Assassinated by the sky,
between the forms that are moving toward the serpent,
and the forms that are moving toward the crystal,
I'll let my hair fall down.

With the tree of amputated limbs that does not sing,
and the boy with the white face of an egg.

With all the tiny animals who have broken heads
and the ragged water that walks on its dry feet.

With all the things that have a deaf and dumb fatigue,
and the butterfly drowned in the inkpot.

Stumbling over my own face that changes every day,
assassinated by the sky!

LORCA IN THE CITY THAT NEVER SLEEPS

Federico Garcia Lorca's *Poet in New York* (*Poeta en Nueva York*) must surely be one of the most misunderstood and under-appreciated books of all time. Written during his troubled sojourn in New York, Vermont and Havana, Cuba, in 1929 and 1930, it was not published during his life (1898–1936) but only in 1940, four years after he was killed by Nationalist militia in Spain. Why did he not publish the book sooner?

Both the subject of these poems and their surrealistic style were foreign to him, that's true enough. However, it's a truth that doesn't really explain anything. Lorca had already made several sweeping changes in style and subject matter in his career, as any artist will do. These changes had led to his popular and critical success with the book *Gypsy Ballads* (*Romancero gitano*, 1928), a reimagining of the poetry and ballads of his native Andalusia. Yet he refused to be typecast in his poetry, his politics or his sexuality. He kept seeking new things to write about and new ways to write about them. Along with his ever-evolving poetry, these creative impulses also found expression in his plays and drawings. These aspects of his artistry would not be fully embraced until after his death, something they have in common with *Poet in New York*.

Some of the poems that would make up the book were published in magazines first. To call the reception they received "mixed" would be putting it mildly. This no doubt contributed to the poet's apparent uncertainty and delay in issuing the book. When *Poet in New York* was finally published posthumously, the negative, dismissive critiques continued and reverberated for several decades.

I have my own theory about this. I think there are three elements at work here. First is the desire to put the artist in a little box called "rural poet of local color." This is the desire of the audience (and more shamefully, of critics) for the artist to keep painting the same picture, playing the same song, writing the same book. The second element of dismissal is more general, a rejection of surrealism overall as a legitimate technique. We are so over this rejection now that we have forgotten it ever occurred. But it did.

Last but not least is that old favorite, the artist and his work being ahead of their time. Again, we tend to forget that this happens frequently.

As long the horse of this ancient, unjust rejection is dead, why don't we go on beating it for a minute? Please bear with me as we dredge up some of these early misbegotten critiques, most of which are hard to lay your hands on these days.

Poems of F. Garcia Lorca (Oxford University Press, 1939), translated by Stephen Spender and J. L. Gili, marked the first major appearance of Lorca's work in English. R. M. Nadal's introduction states about *Poet in New York*: "Although based on sincere feeling, the poem is loaded down with unsophisticated surrealistic extravagances, which, to my mind, spoil what might have been a great work."

The poet's own brother, Francisco Garcia Lorca, wrote in his preface to *Selected Poems of Federico Garcia Lorca* (New Directions, 1955): "If one thing distinguished *Poeta en Nueva York* from all his earlier books, it is the total absence of irony and humor . . ." Well, first of all, that's not even true. There is irony and humor there aplenty if you can accept it wrapped in surrealism, which, obviously, brother Francisco could not. Second, even if it were true, how would that invalidate a work whose primary emotions are shock and horror?

The South African poet and critic Roy Campbell was a complicated character for reasons we don't have time to go into here; still, T. S. Eliot and Dylan Thomas considered him among the best of his generation. His book *Lorca: An Appreciation of His Poetry* (Yale University Press, 1952) is worth tracking down, both for its critical insights and for a number of translations unavailable elsewhere. When it comes to assessing Lorca's New York poems, however, Campbell is just one more literary Helen Keller: "Lorca went and stayed in the U.S.A. for some time, but was unable to establish a real contact with the Americans or their way of life. The result on his poetry was entirely negative. He underwent while there the intellectual influence, if not domination, of Salvador Dali, his friend, who is also a great artist of international repute, but a far more complicated personality than Lorca, more resilient and aggressive, with a far wider range of sympathies and interests, and at home anywhere from the U.S.A. to Catalonia. Lorca attempted to follow the Catalonian into the complex world of surrealism, and lost his depth."

Ouch! It must be admitted that there is a valid point or two in this paragraph. Yet on the whole it underestimates and stereotypes Lorca, a complex person and artist in his own right, with a wide range of sympathies and interests that don't always overlap with those of the more metropolitan Dali. So what?

Within a few short years the critical view of *Poet in New York* had shifted. Angel del Rio explains why in his introduction to *Poet in New York: A New Translation* by Ben Belitt (Grove Press, 1955): ". . . the situation had changed considerably: surrealism had been accepted as an expression of time's restlessness. Moreover, the tragic death of the poet, the defeat of the Spanish Republic and the shadow of war extending over the planet conditioned critic and reader alike to see in these turbulent pieces something more than a meaningless jabber." He then speaks of "the prophetic quality of the book."

Nearly two decades later Robert Bly expressed his unqualified praise for these poems in his commentary in *Selected Poems of Lorca and Jimenez* (Beacon Press, 1973): "The Spanish do not know what to make of *The Poet in New York*, and some critics consider it an aberration, or say flatly that it is exaggerated, or mad. Spain being still largely unindustrialized [note: recall that Bly wrote this half a century ago], they do not realize that it is an understatement. I think it is a marvelous understatement . . ." Bly also says, "His desire-energy becomes bottled up, grows desperate, and bursts out in wild images, poems of desperate power and compassion." He calls the result "still the greatest book ever written about New York." Need I add that I share this view completely?

The surest way to validate this opinion is to get to the poem we'll be looking at today, "Home from a Walk" (also sometimes translated as "Back from a Walk" and "A Walk Around"). My favorite translation of this poem is by Bly. Unfortunately, it does not seem to be readily available online. Several other translations and the Spanish original are available, so hopefully you can make do with them if you don't have Bly's volume of Lorca and Jimenez poems, which, frankly, you should.

The poem begins and ends with the same line, "Assassinated by the sky." There are only twelve lines, four in the first stanza and two in each of the other four stanzas. The poem is shorter than a sonnet and, with its circular structure and each stanza ending with a long "o" sound in the original Spanish, it has its own kind of form. Of course a long "o" sound does not constitute a strict rhyme scheme. Sometimes it's hard *not* to rhyme in Spanish. Additional form comes with the pairing of opposed images in stanzas two through four. Contrary to what the early critics thought, we'll see that the surrealism in these poems is quite apropos and sophisticated.

What a way to start a poem! "Assassinated by the sky." What does it mean? One of the most interesting things about this New York poem is that it doesn't mention a single objective, external, realistic feature of the city. And yet a very specific feeling about it is evoked—disturbing, nightmarish, hallucinatory. I take the opening and closing line to be about the oppression a first-time visitor to the metropolis may feel with this endless procession of skyscrapers looming over him, blocking out much of the accustomed sky. Stanza one continues this oblique approach in its remaining lines:

> between the forms that are moving toward the serpent,
> and the forms that are moving toward the crystal,
> I'll let my hair fall down.

The references to the serpent and the crystal are enigmatic to say the least, strange if not quite surreal. But they are also very clear in a way. How so? Well, imagine you are riding a New York City bus. Would you rather it dropped you off at the serpent or at the crystal? That clarifies things a bit, yes? The last line of stanza one is perhaps Bly's most effective piece of translation here. Other translators have rendered the line as "I'll let my hair grow" or "I'll let my hair grow long" (the latter is how Ben Belitt does it). By putting it the way he does, Bly manages to bring out the tensions of opposites in the poem even more fully in English. Sure, you can let your hair down if it's grown long. The phrase also conveys, though, the idea of speaking freely and frankly, as well as the letting go of inhibitions. In effect, Lorca is giving his muse permission to run wild with surrealism for the next three stanzas.

Each stanza is a couplet beginning with the word "with" and introducing startling pairs of images. The first is "With the tree of amputated limbs that does not sing, / and the boy with the white face of an egg." The first image is of something natural and free cut back to fit into an urban environment. Not to be too literal, but the lack of singing could be ascribed to fewer limbs and fewer leaves to make music of the breeze, as well as fewer birds to make their own music in the tree. This image of something natural cut back contrasts starkly with the image of the egg-faced boy. An egg is something that hasn't been born yet, but here is this "boy" walking around as if he's an adult ready to face the city. He's not. And it may be that Lorca is partly referring to himself with this line.

The third stanza, with the second pair of contrasting surreal images, is: "With all the tiny animals who have broken heads, / and the ragged water that walks on its dry feet." The first image is terrifying, despite being so generic. We have no idea what kinds of animals they are. It's enough to hear that all of their tiny heads are broken, presumably through some type of violence they met with in the city. The opposite of these creatures with a central limb damaged beyond repair is something that shouldn't have any limbs at all, but does, the "ragged water that walks on its dry feet." This monstrous inversion of reality through surrealism turns benign, soothing water into a horror.

Stanza four completes the lineup of contrasting images, and starts to move away from overt surrealism toward naturalism: "With all the things that have a deaf and dumb fatigue, / and the butterfly drowned in the inkpot." With the first image of the couplet, again, we have the very generic "things" suffering from an inarticulate fatigue. It seems these are not creatures but rather inanimate objects, which are not supposed to feel anything, let alone fatigue. The second image of the pair, the "butterfly drowned in the inkpot," seems fairly obvious. Who uses inkpots, after all? The butterfly would appear to be another stand-in for Lorca himself. He's projecting. The implication is that he should not be speechless but he is, overwhelmed by what he experiences on a simple walk about town.

Stanza five, the final one, brings it all home. In the first line once more we have the image of something that should not be and yet is: "Stumbling over my own face that changes every day." How can he be walking on himself? I suppose he could be referring to his shadow. That would give the poem a Jungian tint, which, actually, I believe it does have. I also think he's saying that simply existing in New York is like trampling on your own humanity, your own face. No wonder it changes every day, and no wonder he ends with the same line that began the poem, topped off with an exclamation point for emphasis, "assassinated by the sky!"

I realize this essay is already top-heavy with obscure quotes. Allow me the indulgence of one more from a favorite book, *Within the Context of No Context* by George W. S. Trow. He's responding to a *New York Times Book Review* interview with a woman novelist whose book imagines how the city could be improved. Trow says:

> Her idea was that New York should be *human*. Now, this is simply a mistake. New York is simply an inhuman machine put together to serve the most ambitious of a certain part of American secular society. It has human aspects, because human needs must be met before ambitions can proceed toward realization, but the fulfillment of those needs is an uninteresting precondition of the life of the ambitions. In human terms, there is no reason to live in New York...

That is the city Lorca wrote about so brilliantly, and that is why his New York poems were ahead of their time and probably always will be, like any genuine masterpieces.

Migration

The giant spiders are migrating again.
Their journey is long and perilous
because they can only travel in nightmares.
Last night as I dozed fitfully, two of them
came down the hill, and when they turned off Red Wing Avenue
I was able to blow out some of their dark, bulbous eyes
before the shotgun became black smoke rising from my hands
and a pterodactyl in a bus driver's cap
lifted me screaming into the sky.
Today, as I go about my business—
stamping ALREADY PAID on all of my overdue bills—
I can feel that it is they who sleep uneasily,
relishing yet also fearing our next encounter,
their jaws grinding, their unbearably hairy legs
twitching in anticipation.
This time there will be two shotguns
and a phosphorous grenade, and if all else fails,
a club wrapped in barbed wire at the big end.
Let your remaining eyes look upon that
and tremble, my dreamy darlings . . .

MARY OLIVER

Bone

By Mary Oliver

1.

Understand, I am always trying to figure out
what the soul is,
and where hidden,
and what shape—

and so, last week,
when I found on the beach
the ear bone
of a pilot whale that may have died

hundreds of years ago, I thought
maybe I was close
to discovering something—
for the ear bone

2.

is the portion that lasts longest
in any of us, man or whale; shaped
like a squat spoon
with a pink scoop where

once, in the lively swimmer's head,
it joined its two sisters
in the house of hearing,
it was only

two inches long—
and thought: the soul
might be like this—
so hard, so necessary—

3.

yet almost nothing.
Beside me
the gray sea
was opening and shutting its wave-doors,

unfolding over and over
its time-ridiculing roar;
I looked but I couldn't see anything
through its dark-knit glare;

yet don't we all know, the golden sand
is there at the bottom,
though our eyes have never seen it,
nor can our hands ever catch it

4.

lest we would sift it down
into fractions, and facts—
certainties—
and what the soul is, also

I believe I will never quite know.
Though I play at the edges of knowing,
truly I know
our part is not knowing,

but looking, and touching, and loving,
which is the way I walked on,
softly,
through the pale-pink morning light.

Mary Oliver, Mary Oliver

Everybody loves Mary Oliver (1935–2019). Poets love her, understanding in detail the extent of her accomplishment; and people who know little or nothing about poetry love her, because her work, while full of depths and subtleties, is unpretentious and always accessible. She is said to be the best-selling American poet of recent decades, at a time when the sales of a poetry book often appear to be inversely proportional to the talent of the author. In her universal popularity she resembles Wislawa Szymborska. She could also be called the Beatles of poetry, succeeding commercially because of her obvious charms, but also due to the fact that, underneath, she really is the best of us.

I think it fair to say that, like the Beatles, her fame will only continue to grow, for the simple reason that she is wonderful and she has something we need more than ever: a deep connection with nature, love, and spirit, three things frequently conjoined in her poems. Selecting a Mary Oliver poem to write about is a challenge because it's an embarrassment of riches. She lived a good long time and was quite prolific. As poet and critic James Dickey said of William Stafford, "There are poets who pour out rivers of ink, all on good poems." That certainly applies to Mary Oliver. In fact, the poem we'll be looking at here, "Bone," from her book *Why I Wake Early* (2004), didn't even make it into the final volume of selected poems issued during her lifetime, *Devotions* (2017). Nor has it been overly analyzed. You can easily find it online, as with almost all of her work. One reason I wanted to write about it, though, is that none of those websites reproduce the poem as it appears in her book. Let's begin, shall we?

I think when she originally published the poem in the journal *Shenandoah*, it consisted of four sections, each twelve lines long in a solid block of type, left-aligned. I have no way to verify that because I don't have a copy of that issue and the older issues of the journal are not archived online. But it must be so or all of the websites that have posted the poem would not have followed this form.

When she collected it into the book *Why I Wake Early*, she kept the four sections. Instead of the block type, however, she broke each stanza into three quatrains and centered the type. I think the quatrains are mostly to make the poem more readable and inviting. They are almost entirely unrhymed. Centering the type is something else. In a literal sense, the poem itself is about centering the consciousness around the idea of soul, even if the central point is that Oliver doesn't know what that is. I believe the centering also reflects a degree of concrete poetry, the centered poem visually more resembling the bone found on the beach and the creature in which the bone once lived.

Like so many of her best poems, this one involves an intense, transformative encounter with nature. Yet it begins with the metaphysical. The first word, "Understand"—a plea, a mission, a hope—appears to be addressed equally to the reader and to the author herself:

> Understand, I am always trying to figure out
> what the soul is,
> and where hidden,
> and what shape

The rest of the stanza introduces what she found in one of her beach rambles a week ago, "the ear bone / of a pilot whale," and speculates that the bone may be hundreds of years old. Do you have any idea what the ear bone of a pilot whale looks like? And if you found one on the beach, could you plausibly guess its age? Neither could I. So why do we accept these statements from Oliver? Because she speaks with the casual assurance and quiet authority of one who knows what she's talking about. She gained our trust years ago. When she says something, we tend to go with it.

She continues sharing her knowledge in stanza two, where we learn that the ear bone "is the part that lasts longest / in any of us, man or whale," and that in the case of the whale it is two inches long. And here is where she explicitly connects the physical with the metaphysical:

> [. . .] the soul
> might be like this
> so hard, so necessary

Stanza three begins with the end of that sentence, the end of that thought: "yet almost nothing". There are only three sentences in this poem, and the first one takes up a little more than half of it. Not coincidentally, stanza three is also where the poem turns. Here, for the first time, she brings the sea into it, "opening and shutting its wave-doors" and "unfolding over and over / its time-ridiculing roar". Up until this point she has used alliteration and assonance and an internal rhyme or two. In this stanza she continues these sound patterns and adds to them a couple of end-rhymes and near-rhymes: "me" and "sea"; "doors" and "over" and "roar". All of those "r" sounds make for a pretty convincing reproduction of the ocean's roar. In what sense is that roar "time-ridiculing"? In the sense that time marches on but the ocean is eternal, or seems so to transient creatures like us, and possibly to pilot whales.

The third and final quatrain of stanza three makes an imaginative leap into what might be called informed faith or lived truth:

> yet don't we all know, the golden sand
> is there at the bottom,
> though our eyes have never seen it,
> nor can our hands ever catch it

Having compared the ear bone of the pilot whale to the soul in that both are "so hard, so necessary / yet almost nothing", she now compares the soul to the sand on the ocean floor—even though it's invisible, we know it's there. We could also observe that the soul and the sand have both been made by the actions of something eternal. The second sentence of the poem continues into the final stanza:

> lest we would sift it down
> into fractions, and facts
> certainties
> and what the soul is [. . .]

The second sentence of the poem ends with the first line of the second quatrain of stanza four: "I believe I will never quite know." The quatrain continues, "Though I play at the edges of knowing, / truly I know / our part is not knowing". Like most mystical intuitions, this one embraces and reconciles apparent opposites, things that one might think to be mutually exclusive and contradictory, Oliver's faith in something we can't see, the soul, is balanced by a paradoxical faith in our metaphysical ignorance: we can never know exactly what the soul is. This seems to me a conscious echo of the statement by Yeats, "Man can embody truth but he cannot know it."

What is our part then? The final quatrain of the final stanza sums it up nicely but not too neatly:

> [. . .] looking, and touching, and loving,
>   which is the way I walked on,
>   softly,
> through the pale-pink morning light.

I think it's meaningful that only two lines in this poem consist of single words, and they're both here in stanza four, "certainties," the third line of the first quatrain, and "softly," the third line of the third and final quatrain. The hardness of certainty balances against the softness of faith. Yet, oddly, faith is not completely soft as it turns out. It can be as hard as a grain of sand or the ear bone of a pilot whale. All of those "w" sounds in the second line of the final quatrain serve as a reminder of the whale that started the poem: "which is the way I walked on." And of course one is never surprised to find Mary Oliver looking up at the morning light.

What surprises us is how readily we accept her ruminations and pronouncements, offered however tentatively, on these invisible and inchoate matters. We accept what she says because we know we are in the presence of one who knows. And the sign of her knowledge, ironically, is that she is a kind of poetic Socrates, quicker to say what she doesn't know. This is why we trust Mary Oliver, and also why we love her.

Cottonwood Seeds

A million of them weigh less than three pounds.
No wonder they lift away on the wind,
miniature paratroopers buoyed by filaments
finer than a spider's web and carried
for miles in search of water.
The actual seed is barely visible
to the naked eye, yet each one contains
complete instructions for assembling
a tree that may reach a hundred feet
into the blue air, growing fast
though only lasting so long.
Chances are, if you planted one as a child
you have already outlived it.
But the leaves! The leaves are shining
green diamonds that shimmer in the slightest
breeze, their long stems giving them
unusual freedom of movement for prisoners.
Their rustling reminds me of a harem chamber,
the sound of silks on silks, flesh on flesh . . .
and now my mind is wandering
farther than any seed borne on the wind.
This image too is somehow latent
and lurking in the cottonwood seed,
worlds sleeping within worlds asleep,
tiny travelers suddenly bursting forth
by the billions to make it snow in June, in us.

LEWIS CARROLL

Jabberwocky

By Lewis Carroll

'Twas brillig, and the slithy toves
    Did gyre and gimble in the wabe:
All mimsy were the borogoves,
    And the mome raths outgrabe.

"Beware the Jabberwock, my son!
    The jaws that bite, the claws that catch!
Beware the Jubjub bird, and shun
    The frumious Bandersnatch!"

He took his vorpal sword in hand;
    Long time the manxome foe he sought—
So rested he by the Tumtum tree
    And stood awhile in thought.

And, as in uffish thought he stood,
    The Jabberwock, with eyes of flame,
Came whiffling through the tulgey wood,
    And burbled as it came!

One, two! One, two! And through and through
    The vorpal blade went snicker-snack!
He left it dead, and with its head
    He went galumphing back.

"And hast thou slain the Jabberwock?
    Come to my arms, my beamish boy!
O frabjous day! Callooh! Callay!"
    He chortled in his joy.

'Twas brillig, and the slithy toves
    Did gyre and gimble in the wabe:
All mimsy were the borogoves,
    And the mome raths outgrabe.

HERE WE COME A-LEWIS CARROLLING, OR: SOME SENSIBLE THOUGHTS ON THE NONSENSE OF "JABBERWOCKY"

What is the most famous nonsense poem in the English language? If you guessed "The Waste Land" by T. S. Eliot, or "Leaving the Atocha Station" by John Ashbery, or "oxygen" by Aram Saroyan, or any of various mid-twentieth-century American billboards featuring Burma Shave, you'd be close but no cigar. The hands-down winner, as declared unanimously by the judges (me and history), is "Jabberwocky" by Lewis Carroll, aka Charles Dodgson (1832–1898).

The poem first appeared in 1871 in *Through the Looking-Glass, and What Alice Found There*, the sequel to *Alice's Adventures in Wonderland* (1865). Those two books and the mock-epic poem *The Hunting of the Snark* constitute the entire basis of Carroll's literary reputation, and they are more than enough. "Jabberwocky" is a highlight of *Through the Looking-Glass* and has come to have a life of its own, inspiring any number of tributes, imitations and references in the century and a half since it first greeted the world. To wit:

In 1968 a British studio group released a silly psychedelic pop single called "Jabberwock," backed with "Which Dreamed It." Both songs were adapted from Carroll poems, as was the group's name, Boeing Duveen and the Beautiful Soup. The leader was Sam Hutt, in real life a physician and friend of Pink Floyd, and the record was produced by a young Tony Visconti, before he became David Bowie's frequent collaborator. You can find the songs on YouTube or in the second box of the *Rubble* collection.

Donovan wrote his own musical backing for "Jabberwocky" and released it on one of his least-known albums, *HMS Donovan* (1971). This double-LP collection of children's songs also includes a version of Carroll's "The Walrus and the Carpenter" and "The Owl and the Pussycat" by Carroll's main competitor in the nonsense verse sweepstakes, Edward Lear. Of course, given today's declining educational standards, these song-poems are over the heads of most adults, let alone children.

Saturday Night Live was still in its first season on February 21, 1976, when Desi Arnaz hosted Episode 14. He proved to be quite good at it. There are many great moments, such as his performance of the songs "Cuban Pete" and "Babalu" with son Desi Arnaz, Jr. (late of Dino, Desi and Billy). But the best sequence is when he recites "Jabberwocky" in that cockeyed Cuban accent of his, seeming to improvise his own jokes and comments. There is something very moving about seeing this nineteenth-century classic lovingly manhandled by one of the comedic icons of 1950s television as he passes the torch to the Not Ready for Primetime Players, who would determine the course of comedy for the next few decades, and even now.

The following year, Terry Gilliam made his solo directorial debut with *Jabberwocky*, a rambunctious if uneven film that appeared to want to carry on where *Monty Python and the Holy Grail* had left off. Only loosely based on the Carroll poem, it featured Gilliam, Terry Jones and "Seventh Python" Neil Innes in smaller roles, with Michael Palin in the lead. While it probably did not cause Carroll to spin in his grave, neither was it likely to help him sleep the big sleep more peacefully.

I could go on. I could tell you what *The Muppet Show* did with the poem in 1980 (very clever actually), but you get the point. "Jabberwocky" is here to stay. It has woven itself into our culture, high and low. I haven't even mentioned its effect on other writers, such as James Joyce. We might as well get on with appreciating why it keeps resonating with us in so many ways.

Carroll began the poem in 1855, finishing the first stanza and sharing it with his family. Even in this larval form it is a powerful bit of fun:

> 'Twas brillig, and the slithy toves
>   Did gyre and gimble in the wabe:
> All mimsy were the borogoves,
>   And the mome raths outgrabe.

The first thing one notices is the abundance of nonce words, invented words. By my count there are ten of them in this stanza alone. As Alice says after reading the whole poem, "Somehow it seems to fill my head with ideas—only I don't know exactly what they are!" And that is what the author intended, intentional fallacy be damned. Though we can't know precisely what is happening, it is somewhat ominous and dreadful, partly, perhaps, for that very reason. Those "slithy toves" sound perfectly awful, and I have no wish to see them "gimble in the wabe." I have no idea what the "mome raths" are, but I'm pretty sure I don't ever want them to "outgrabe" me.

This first stanza contains the most notable use of the word "gyre" in English verse until Yeats resurrected it for his own "The Second Coming." Come to think of it, his "rough beast . . . slouching towards Bethlehem to be born" owes more than a little to the Jabberwock. Both poems play on our dread, one for humor, the other for horror.

Back to you, Mr. Carroll! At this early stage he titled the fragment "Stanza of Anglo-Saxon Poetry." It does indeed sound medieval. One scholar also heard echoes of Shakespeare in it—specifically a passage in Act I Scene 1 of *Hamlet*, where "the sheeted dead / Did squeak and gibber in the Roman streets." However, I don't mean to go down the rabbit hole with Alice and get lost in all of the possible sources of the poem. The point is, whatever odds and ends were rattling around in Carroll's well-read head, this is what came out. As with any poem worth reading, it must stand on its own two scaly feet. On to stanza two:

"Beware the Jabberwock, my son!
    The jaws that bite, the claws that catch!
Beware the Jubjub bird, and shun
    The frumious Bandersnatch!"

Remember when I promised to stop bringing up pop culture references to the poem? Well, I lied. I have to mention that Frumious Bandersnatch was the name of a Berkeley-based sixties psychedelic group whose members would later become part of the Steve Miller Band and Journey.

By the way, who is speaking in this stanza? He calls our unnamed hero "son," but is he really his father? Or perhaps his father confessor? Priests often do have prominent roles in medieval literature. Unfortunately, without a DNA test we'll never know.

Regardless, this stanza serves to introduce the titular monster. And, though we haven't mentioned the actual poetry of the poem yet, there is quite a bit of it in these first two stanzas. They are composed of quatrains with an ABAB rhyme scheme and an iambic meter. There are generally eight syllables per line, except for the last line, which has six (the end line of stanza two has seven syllables, making it the lone exception in the poem). We have alliteration aplenty: "gyre and gimble"; "mimsy" and "mome"; "Jaberwock," "jaws," "Jubjub"; "claws" and "catch." I could only locate one clear instance of assonance: "Jubjub" and "shun."

Stanza three finds our anonymous protagonist about to engage the beast, only he suddenly decides to pull a Hamlet:

> He took his vorpal blade in hand;
>   Longtime the manxsome foe he sought—
> So rested he by the Tumtum tree
>   And stood awhile in thought.

After all, it's only a Jabberwock on the loose. We can afford to take a little rest break by the Tumtum tree, yes? Another thing to notice here is the departure from the rhyme scheme we started with. This stanza is ABCB. Further, because C doesn't rhyme with A, Carroll gives it an internal rhyme with "he" and "tree".

Now we get to the main action in stanzas four and five:

> And, as in uffish thought he stood,
>   The Jabberwock, with eyes of flame,
> Came whiffling through the tulgey wood,
>   And burbled as it came!

> One, two! One, two! And through and through
>   The vorpal blade went snicker-snack!
> He left it dead, and with its head
>   He went galumphing back.

Stanza four returns to the original rhyme scheme of ABAB. Stanza five uses the ABCB scheme of stanza three, with another internal rhyme in C, "dead" and "head." "Uffish" certainly sounds like a close relative of "oafish." "Eyes of flame" strongly suggests that we are dealing with some sort of dragon. As for the last line of stanza four, I have known several creatures who burbled as they came, but this is a family publication. "Galumphing" is one of several nonce words coined for the poem that have since become neologisms, that is to say, words fully accepted into the language, with their own dictionary entries and everything. At any rate, despite his dawdling and diffidence our hero has managed to kill and decapitate the Jabberwock. And in the penultimate stanza, number six, he receives a hero's welcome:

> "And hast thou slain the Jabberwock?
> Come to my arms, my beamish boy!
> O frabjous day! Callooh! Callay!"
> He chortled in his joy.

Again he employs the ABCB rhyme scheme with an internal rhyme in C. The last line gives us another nonce word, "chortled," that has become a neologism. In fact, I use it in one of my two tribute poems to "Jabberwocky" below. Carroll may have thought he was coining the word "beamish," though it has its own obscure, respectable lineage. There is no question that he coined "frabjous" and "callooh" and "callay," which are wonderful words. If we all keep using them, they too will enter the language as this poem has entered our culture.

Carroll could have easily ended the poem there. Instead, he repeats stanza one, making the poem into a circular journey, what in his time might have been described as a Sisyphean struggle, or in ours as a time loop. The implication is that there is always another Jabberwock, or a Jubjub bird, or a frumious Bandersnatch, just as in *Buffy the Vampire Slayer* there is always another apocalypse.

As is the way of most classics, "Jabberwocky" has influenced generations of writers of all types. I mentioned Joyce and Yeats. I would also say that authors as diverse as Jorge Luis Borges, Kurt Vonnegut, P. G. Wodehouse, Gertrude Stein, Thomas Pynchon and the whole New York School of poets have taken much of value from Lewis Carroll, aside from the pure pleasure his work offers.

At the beginning of this essay I made light of what I consider a completely impenetrable poem by John Ashbery, "Leaving the Atocha Station," from what some readers would agree is his most difficult, confounding book, *The Tennis Court Oath*. Yet with a slightly less extreme application of the same techniques, learned in part from "nonsense" poems such as "Jabberwocky," Ashbery and his compatriots created some masterpieces too. And that is one more reason to be grateful to Mr. Carroll for bringing forth his burbling beast.

A Nonsense Verse

(Unfortunately, Not Written by Lewis Carroll or Edward Lear)

When men were men, and women were men,
And the rest of us were trying to rest,
They picked a number from one to ten
But which they picked is anyone's guess.

For on a spinning top there stands
A man whose face could use a rinse,
And coiling slyly in his hands
Are miles and miles of fingerprints.

Yet there is hope for those who sneeze
And those who drive the Shriner's car:
If half the locks fit half the keys
Then maybe the jam will fit the jar.

A Literary Limerick

A gentleman named T. S. Eliot
Is heaven's wittiest man of belles lettres.
 "I think I'm immortal,"
 He says with a chortle,
"But God knows it's too early to tell yet."

KENNETH KOCH

Fresh Air

By Kenneth Koch

I

At the Poem Society a black-haired man stands up to say
"You make me sick with all your talk about restraint and mature talent!
Haven't you ever looked out the window at a painting by Matisse,
Or did you always stay in hotels where there were too many spiders crawling
    on your visages?
Did you ever glance inside a bottle of sparkling pop,
Or see a citizen split in two by the lightning?
I am afraid you have never smiled at the hibernation
Of bear cubs except that you saw in it some deep relation
To human suffering and wishes, oh what a bunch of crackpots!"
The black-haired man sits down, and the others shoot arrows at him.
A blond man stands up and says,
"He is right! Why should we be organized to defend the kingdom
Of dullness? There are so many slimy people connected with poetry,
Too, and people who know nothing about it!
I am not recommending that poets like each other and organize to fight
    them,
But simply that lightning should strike them."
Then the assembled mediocrities shot arrows at the blond-haired man.
The chairman stood up on the platform, oh he was physically ugly!
He was small-limbed and -boned and thought he was quite seductive,
But he was bald with certain hideous black hairs,
And his voice had the sound of water leaving a vaseline bathtub,
And he said, "The subject for this evening's discussion is poetry
On the subject of love between swans." And everyone threw candy hearts
At the disgusting man, and they stuck to his bib and tucker,
And he danced up and down on the platform in terrific glee
And recited the poetry of his little friends—but the blond man stuck his head
Out of a cloud and recited poems about the east and thunder,
And the black-haired man moved through the stratosphere chanting
Poems of the relationships between terrific prehistoric charcoal whales,

And the slimy man with candy hearts sticking all over him
Wilted away like a cigarette paper on which the bumblebees have urinated,
And all the professors left the room to go back to their duty,
And all that were left in the room were five or six poets
And together they sang the new poem of the twentieth century
Which, though influenced by Mallarmé, Shelley, Byron, and Whitman,
Plus a million other poets, is still entirely original
And is so exciting that it cannot be here repeated.
You must go to the Poem Society and wait for it to happen.
Once you have heard this poem you will not love any other,
Once you have dreamed this dream you will be inconsolable,
Once you have loved this dream you will be as one dead,
Once you have visited the passages of this time's great art!

2

"Oh to be seventeen years old
Once again," sang the red-haired man, "and not know that poetry
Is ruled with the sceptre of the dumb, the deaf, and the creepy!"
And the shouting persons battered his immortal body with stones
And threw his primitive comedy into the sea
From which it sang forth poems irrevocably blue.

Who are the great poets of our time, and what are their names?
Yeats of the baleful influence, Auden of the baleful influence, Eliot of the
    baleful influence
(Is Eliot a great poet? no one knows), Hardy, Stevens, Williams (is Hardy of
    our time?),
Hopkins (is Hopkins of our time?), Rilke (is Rilke of our time?), Lorca (is
    Lorca of our time?), who is still of our time?
Mallarmé, Valéry, Apollinaire, Éluard, Reverdy, French poets are still of our
    time,
Pasternak and Mayakovsky, is Jouve of our time?

Where are young poets in America, they are trembling in publishing houses
    and universities,

Above all they are trembling in universities, they are bathing the library steps with their spit,
They are gargling out innocuous (to whom?) poems about maple trees and their children,
Sometimes they brave a subject like the Villa d'Este or a lighthouse in Rhode Island,
Oh what worms they are! they wish to perfect their form.
Yet could not these young men, put in another profession,
Succeed admirably, say at sailing a ship? I do not doubt it, Sir, and I wish we could try them.
(A plane flies over the ship holding a bomb but perhaps it will not drop the bomb,
The young poets from the universities are staring anxiously at the skies,
Oh they are remembering their days on the campus when they looked up to watch birds excrete,
They are remembering the days they spent making their elegant poems.)

Is there no voice to cry out from the wind and say what it is like to be the wind,
To be roughed up by the trees and to bring music from the scattered houses
And the stones, and to be in such intimate relationship with the sea
That you cannot understand it? Is there no one who feels like a pair of pants?

3

Summer in the trees! "It is time to strangle several bad poets."
The yellow hobbyhorse rocks to and fro, and from the chimney
Drops the Strangler! The white and pink roses are slightly agitated by the struggle,
But afterwards beside the dead "poet" they cuddle up comfortingly against their vase. They are safer now, no one will compare them to the sea.

Here on the railroad train, one more time, is the Strangler.
He is going to get that one there, who is on his way to a poetry reading.
Agh! Biff! A body falls to the moving floor.

In the football stadium I also see him,

He leaps through the frosty air at the maker of comparisons
Between football and life and silently, silently strangles him!

Here is the Strangler dressed in a cowboy suit
Leaping from his horse to annihilate the students of myth!

The Strangler's ear is alert for the names of Orpheus,
Cuchulain, Gawain, and Odysseus,
And for poems addressed to Jane Austen, F. Scott Fitzgerald,
To Ezra Pound, and to personages no longer living
Even in anyone's thoughts—O Strangler the Strangler!

He lies on his back in the waves of the Pacific Ocean.

4

Supposing that one walks out into the air
On a fresh spring day and has the misfortune
To encounter an article on modern poetry
In *New World Writing*, or has the misfortune
To see some examples of some of the poetry
Written by the men with their eyes on the myth
And the Missus and the midterms, in the *Hudson Review*,
Or, if one is abroad, in *Botteghe Oscure*,
Or indeed in *Encounter*, what is one to do
With the rest of one's day that lies blasted to ruins
All bluely about one, what is one to do?
O surely one cannot complain to the President,
Nor even to the deans of Columbia College,
Nor to T. S. Eliot, nor to Ezra Pound,
And supposing one writes to the Princess Caetani,
"Your poets are awful!" what good would it do?
And supposing one goes to the *Hudson Review*
With a package of matches and sets fire to the building?
One ends up in prison with trial subscriptions
To the *Partisan, Sewanee,* and *Kenyon Review*!

5

Sun out! perhaps there is a reason for the lack of poetry
In these ill-contented souls, perhaps they need air!
Blue air, fresh air, come in, I welcome you, you are an art student,
Take off your cap and gown and sit down on the chair.
Together we shall paint the poets—but no, air! perhaps you should go to them, quickly,
Give them a little inspiration, they need it, perhaps they are out of breath,
Give them a little inhuman company before they freeze the English language to death!
(And rust their typewriters a little, be sea air! be noxious! kill them, if you must, but stop their poetry!
I remember I saw you dancing on the surf on the Côte d'Azur,
And I stopped, taking my hat off, but you did not remember me,
Then afterwards you came to my room bearing a handful of orange flowers
And we were together all through the summer night!)

That we might go away together, it is so beautiful on the sea, there are a few white clouds in the sky!

But no, air! you must go . . . Ah, stay!

But she has departed and . . . Ugh! what poisonous fumes and clouds! what a suffocating atmosphere!
Cough! whose are these hideous faces I see, what is this rigor
Infecting the mind? where are the green Azores,
Fond memories of childhood, and the pleasant orange trolleys,
A girl's face, red-white, and her breasts and calves, blue eyes, brown eyes, green eyes, fahrenheit
Temperatures, dandelions, and trains, O blue?!
Wind, wind, what is happening? Wind! I can't see any bird but the gull, and I feel it should symbolize . . .
Oh, pardon me, there's a swan, one two three swans, a great white swan, hahaha how pretty they are! Smack!
Oh! stop! help! yes, I see—disrespect for my superiors—forgive me, dear Zeus, nice Zeus, parabolic bird, O feathered excellence! white!

There is Achilles too, and there's Ulysses, I've always wanted to see them,
And there is Helen of Troy, I suppose she is Zeus too, she's so terribly pretty—hello, Zeus, my you are beautiful, Bang!
One more mistake and I get thrown out of the Modern Poetry Association, help! Why aren't there any adjectives around?
Oh there are, there's practically nothing else—look, here's *grey, utter, agonized, total, phenomenal, gracile, invidious, sundered,* and *fused, Elegant, absolute, pyramidal,* and . . . Scream! but what can I describe with these words? States!
States symbolized and divided by two, complex states, magic states, states of consciousness governed by an aroused sincerity, cockadoodle doo!
Another bird! is it morning? Help! where am I? am I in the barnyard? oink oink, scratch, moo! Splash!
My first lesson. "Look around you. What do you think and feel?" *Uhhh* . . . "Quickly!" *This Connecticut landscape would have pleased Vermeer.* Wham! A-Plus. "Congratulations!" I am promoted.
OOOhhhhh I wish I were dead, what a headache! My second lesson: "Rewrite your first lesson line six hundred times. Try to make it into a magnetic field." I can do it too. But my poor line! What a nightmare! Here comes a tremendous horse,
Trojan, I presume. No, it's my third lesson. "Look, look! Watch him, see what he's doing? That's what we want you to do. Of course it won't be the same as his at first, but . . ." I demur. Is there no other way to fertilize minds?
Bang! I give in . . . Already I see my name in two or three anthologies, a serving girl comes into the barn bringing me the anthologies,
She is very pretty and I smile at her a little sadly, perhaps it is my last smile! Perhaps she will hit me! But no, she smiles in return, and she takes my hand.
My hand, my hand! what is this strange thing I feel in my hand, on my arm, on my chest, my face—can it be . . . ? it is! AIR!
Air, air, you've come back! Did you have any success? "What do you think?" I don't know, air. You are so strong, air.
And she breaks my chains of straw, and we walk down the road, behind us the hideous fumes!

Soon we reach the seaside, she is a young art student who places her head on my shoulder,
I kiss her warm red lips, and here is the Strangler, reading the *Kenyon Review*! Good luck to you, Strangler!
Goodbye, Helen! goodbye, fumes! goodbye, abstracted dried-up boys! goodbye, dead trees! goodbye, skunks!
Goodbye, manure! goodbye, critical manicure! goodbye, you big fat men standing on the east coast as well as the west giving poems the test! farewell, Valéry's stern dictum!
Until tomorrow, then, scum floating on the surface of poetry! goodbye for a moment, refuse that happens to land in poetry's boundaries! adieu, stale eggs teaching imbeciles poetry to bolster up your egos! adios, boring anomalies of these same stale eggs!
Ah, but the scum is deep! Come, let me help you! and soon we pass into the clear blue water. Oh GOODBYE, castrati of poetry! farewell, stale pale skunky pentameters (the only honest English meter, gloop gloop!) until tomorrow, horrors! oh, farewell!

Hello, sea! good morning, sea! hello, clarity and excitement, you great expanse of green—

O green, beneath which all of them shall drown!

STILL FRESH AND FUNNY AFTER ALL THESE YEARS: THE ENDURING SUBVERSIVE CHARM OF KENNETH KOCH'S BIGGEST AND MOST SERIOUS JOKE

I'm tired of thinking about poetry.

Let's stop here by this cool mountain stream and consider instead how some of the great screeds of history could be improved by the judicious application of humor. For example, take Martin Luther's *95 Theses*, surely the most popular screed to be nailed to the door of All Saints' Church in Wittenberg, Germany, in 1517. But, let's face it, if you weren't in the burning-heretics-at-the-stake business, this document was pretty dull and dreary stuff. What if he had named it *96 Theses* and if number 96 was: "Be it hereby revealed in Holy Writ and divine revelation that Mrs. Luther's blueberry pies are more scrumptious than anything available in the Vatican Bake Shoppe." His point would've been made, the Reformation still would've happened, yet possibly without bloodshed and with much better desserts.

Or take this gem in *Quotations from Chairman Mao Tse-Tung* (aka *The Little Red Book*): "Learn to 'play the piano.' In playing the piano, all ten fingers are in motion; it will not do to move some fingers and not the others." What if he had changed it to: "Learn to 'play the piano' like Chico Marx." Quite possibly the Cultural Revolution might have taken a different turn, and China could have spared itself the deaths of tens of millions due to political purges and the implementation of Mao's insane ideas on socialist agriculture.

I could go on. Anyway, you get the point. Contrary to what Mary Poppins says, it's not a spoonful of sugar that makes the medicine go down, but rather a dollop of humor. Which brings us to the most famous screed in the history of poetry, "Fresh Air" by Kenneth Koch. This full-frontal assault on the failed verse of the time was written in 1956 and published in the poet's 1962 volume *Thank You and Other Poems* (Evergreen). Koch performed it at many readings and it was certainly infamous long before it was put into a book (the poem was rejected by *Poetry* and *Partisan Review*, and finally accepted by *i.e., The Cambridge Review*).

The most amazing thing about the poem is how it combines a truly savage attack on bad contemporary poetry with large helpings of humor and genuine lyricism. It manages to authoritatively condemn inferior work while offering an example of superior work and loads of laughs. It is not simply an angry polemic (though make no mistake, there is plenty of anger in it). As all great literature should be, it is first and foremost tremendously engaging and entertaining. Let's look at how Koch achieved that.

The poem is in five parts, numbered, not named. It begins with an imaginary scene:

> At the Poem Society a black-haired man stands up to say
> "You make me sick with all your talk about restraint and mature talent!
> Haven't you ever looked out the window at a painting by Matisse,
> Or did you always stay in hotels where there were too many spiders crawling
>   on your visages?
> Did you ever glance inside a bottle of sparking pop,
> Or see a citizen split in two by the lightning?
> I am afraid you have never smiled at the hibernation
> Of bear cubs except that you see in it some deep relation
> To human suffering and wishes, oh what a bunch of crackpots!"

Now that is another "Shot Heard 'Round the World"! Not as deadly as the bullets fired at Lexington and Concord, perhaps, but every bit as revolutionary, and ultimately just as fatal to the literary fatuities of the moment. He writes in a long free-verse line clearly inspired by Whitman, as Allen Ginsberg was doing at exactly the same time. The exclamation points are also Whitmanesque, as they are in Ginsberg's work. I know comparisons are odious, but if I may make one—I often feel that Ginsberg throws in exclamation points to try to whip up an excitement that is not actually present in the poet or the poem, whereas the same exclamation points erupt from a Koch poem because of an authentic excitement that cannot be contained. Long before Warren Zevon popularized the term, Koch was the original Excitable Boy.

Another thing to notice about the opening volley of these first nine lines: the ghastly "Poem Society" would appear to be a stand-in for a nonfictional organization. My first guess was the Modern Poetry Association (MPA), the former publisher of *Poetry* magazine. It was founded in 1941 and was only fifteen years old when Koch wrote this. However, he mentions the MPA by name near the end of the poem. So here he must be making fun of the Academy of American Poets, founded in 1934.

As he does throughout the poem, Koch mixes drop-dead funny jokes ("Or did you always stay in hotels where there were too many spiders crawling on your visages?") with moments of surprising lyricism. When he asks, "Haven't you ever looked out the window at a painting by Matisse," is he saying that it takes the eye of an artist to perceive potential art in every mundane moment? Or does he mean that reality is constantly supplying us with visions of boundless beauty and wonder all around us all the time, comparable to the work of our best artists? It's a striking phrase any way you look at it. Of course it is also a reminder that the New York School poets saw themselves as leading a literary revolution that followed in the wake of great painters.

Two other seemingly straightforward lines—"Did you ever glance inside a bottle of sparkling pop, / Or see a citizen split in two by the lightning?"—also contain layers of meaning. Koch is an inveterate celebrator of the simple pleasures of everyday American life, such as baseball and pop. But notice how he refers to the pop. He invites us to glance inside it, not merely at it, which would show the bubbles of carbonation forming and releasing, and at the same bring our ears close enough to hear the fizz. Thus the image contains a hidden sound. And then he leaps right into the image of "a citizen split in two by the lightning."

The first section of the poem takes place at a meeting of the Poem Society. An argument is already underway as we come on the scene, an argument about what modern poetry is versus what it should be. Koch didn't have to recap what was going on in poetry in 1956, because his fellow poets were well aware of it. Still, it may be helpful to remind a contemporary audience of what the issues were. Poets born in the last decades of the nineteenth century—Yeats, Pound, Eliot, Williams, H. D. and all the rest—had wrought a revolution in poetry in the first decades of the twentieth century. It had been a total war, organized by Pound more than anyone else, and victory had been total as well. As always happens, though, victory brings its own problems. The former revolutionaries become the new establishment.

Instead of following the excellent advice from Pound to "make it new," many poets opted to make it like Pound, and Eliot, and the other leaders of the revolution. After all, imitation is the sincerest form of plagiarism.

At the same time as most poets were failing in their creative duties (which, to be honest, is what most poets are doing most of the time in any age), the literary world was tilting toward critics as if literature was really something to do with them, as opposed to writers and readers. William Empson's book *Seven Types of Ambiguity* became the cornerstone of the New Criticism, along with *The Well Wrought Urn* by Cleanth Brooks. So pernicious was the influence of these noxious tomes that writers started using them as blueprints for their work. The most pathetic example was Robert Lowell, for many years regarded as one of the best poets in the country. If you are in any degree a fan of Lowell, you'd better step away from this essay now, because in my view if you threw his entire life's work into the mouth of an active volcano, our literature would be vastly improved.

Even Eliot took part in this madness, claiming that it was the poet's job to provide an "objective correlative" to impart his or her vision to the reader. What rubbish! Eliot never once in his life sat down at his desk trying to think of an objective correlative. The only American author who might've had the intellect to approach the job that way would've been Henry James. And in the end he was just like the rest of us: staring at the blank page while shudders of horror and desperation wracked his frame, sweating blood until he managed to come up with something he hoped was new. In his case, it usually was. Would that all of us were so fortunate.

Back to the poem! We haven't even made it through the first part. Here's a bit more of that:

> A blond man stands up and says,
> "He is right! Why should we be organized to defend the kingdom
> Of dullness? There are so many slimy people connected with poetry,
> Too, and people who know nothing about it!
> I am not recommending that poets like each other and organize to fight them,
>
> But simply that lightning should strike them.

There follows a kind poetry slam between the chairman of the Poem Society—an ugly little man whose voice "had the sound of water leaving a vaseline bathtub"—and the black-haired man, the blond man and half a dozen of their friends. It's no contest. At the end of it, the chairman "Wilted away like a cigarette paper on which the bumblebees have urinated." The meeting adjourns and the other poets can't help but go on singing:

> And together they sang the new poem of the twentieth century,
> Which, though influenced by Mallarme, Shelley, Byron, and Whitman,
> Plus a million other poets, is still entirely original
> And is so exciting that it cannot be here repeated.

This would be a good place to mention the lack of critical appreciation and approval for Koch, both during and after the formative years of the New York School and for some time after. In a way this withholding of recognition applied to the whole movement. Yet it applied even more to Koch for one simple, silly reason. As Koch's student Ron Padgett explained in his introduction to Koch's *Selected Poems* (Library of America 2006), "In the dominant atmosphere of the somewhat depressed and solemn academic poetry of the 1950s and '60s Koch had been, after all, a disarming rarity: a highly sophisticated and serious comic poet." This comment is still more perceptive and profound than it might appear. How many readers are even aware that a comic poet can be serious, despite the examples of much of the work of Shakespeare, Byron, Wilde, Pound and Cummings? Precious few is the not at all amusing answer.

One example of the critical dismissal of Koch can be found in the otherwise excellent volume *Alone with America: Essays on the Art of Poetry in the United States Since 1950* (1969) by poet and critic Richard Howard. The book was a rare work of poetic criticism that was really about the poems, not the critic. It greatly enhanced our understanding of an entire generation of poets that, up until then, had been underappreciated. In it, Howard examines the work of the three best-known (at that time) New York School poets, Ashbery, O'Hara and Koch. He undervalues all of them, but for Koch he cannot seem to utter a single kind word. Not that he denigrates him directly either. Here is the phrase that really sticks in my craw: "This outcry is from Koch's rhetorical manifesto 'Fresh Air,' a screed which explains, or at least explodes, the fallacies of all other poets except Kenneth Koch." As we have seen from the passages of the poem already quoted, this is a damnable lie. Koch is very quick, even eager, to credit the many inspirations and antecedents for the poetry that he and his friends were writing.

This is even more apparent in the second part of the poem, which begins with this ginger outcry:

> "Oh to be seventeen years old
> Once again," sang the red-haired man, "and not know that poetry
> Is ruled with the scepter of the dumb, the deaf, and the creepy!"

There follows another litany of poets, this time asking hard questions and starting to make important distinctions between poets whose work is useful to those of us writing in the present, and poets whose work is not useful to us:

> Who are the great poets of our time, and what are their names?
> Yeats of the baleful influence, Auden of the baleful influence, Eliot of the baleful influence
> (Is Eliot a great poet? no one knows), Hardy, Stevens, Williams (is Hardy of our time?),
> Hopkins (is Hopkins of our time?), Rilke (is Rilke of our time?), Lorca (is Lorca of our time?), who is still of our time?
> Mallarmé, Valéry, Apollinaire, Éluard, Reverdy, French poets are still of our time,
> Pasternak and Mayakovsky, is Jouve still of our time?

Let me admit here, I never heard the name of French poet Pierre Jean Jouve before reading this poem, though he was nominated five times for a Nobel Prize. In any case, this passage puts forth the idea that a poet can be great yet not of our time, and thus, not so useful to us. For the record, the question of whether Eliot is a great poet is one that Eliot himself could not answer. In an interview with the *Paris Review* in 1959, when asked whether he was assured of his reputation, he said something like no, and how could anyone be so assured (I don't have it in front of me)?

Interestingly, Koch does not question whether Stevens or Williams are still of our time, nor does he accuse them of having a baleful influence. At the time he wrote this Stevens had just died. Williams died in 1963, one year after this poem was collected into a book.

Also in 1963, Robert Bly published his own screed, an essay called "A Wrong Turning in American Poetry," in the Chicago-based magazine

Choice. It too is a powerful critique of the effete, denatured, academic verse so common in the fifties. Bly goes Koch one better (or worse) by naming contemporaries. The American poetry scene was much smaller then, with far fewer periodicals, and only a handful that really mattered. The essay caused a scandal and a sensation in a way that would be impossible today. Every poet in the country read it, terrified of finding themselves mentioned in it. Bly made himself some lifelong enemies with it, which of course is bound to happen when you take a stand, any stand. One difference between Bly's essay and Koch's poem is that there are many cruel smiles in the essay but no laughs. Also, Bly seeks inspiration more in the Hispanic and German-speaking poets than in the French. As far as he's concerned, Lorca and Rilke are certainly of our time. He further name-checks Pablo Neruda and Juan Ramon Jimenez, among others. The essay deserves to be revisited on the occasion of its sixtieth anniversary. And I mean to do that at another place and time. The only other thing to say about it here is that it almost completely and unfairly ignores the work of the New York School poets.

As part two of the poem barrels to a close, Koch asks plaintively, "Where are young poets in America, they are trembling in publishing houses and universities." A little further on, he exclaims, "Oh what worms they are! they wish to perfect their form." The final stanza of part two yearns for some genuine poetry while simultaneously offering us some:

> Is there no voice to cry out from the wind and say what it is like to be the wind,
> To be roughed up by the trees and bring music from the scattered houses
> Of the stones, and to be in such intimate relationship with the sea
> That you cannot understand it? Is there no one who feels like a pair of pants?

Those last two lines are particularly good. First he reminds us that if we knew anything about the sea we would know how little we know. Then he brings us back down to earth with the thought that poetry also lives in the wonderful mundanity of a pair of pants. Love that!

In part three of "Fresh Air" Koch fantasizes most delightfully about the prospect of taking violent personal action against bad poetry. It begins: "Summer in the trees. 'It is time to strangle several bad poets.' " And then the Strangler—a stand-in for Koch, no doubt—comes down the chimney like Santa Claus and throttles a versifier who clearly has it coming. There are white and pink roses in the room that are "slightly agitated by the struggle." On the bright side, "They are safe now, no one will compare them to the sea."

The penultimate section of the poem, part four, is the shortest. Koch uses it to lampoon some of the leading poetry outlets of his time. I find it fascinating that nearly seven decades later most of them are still with us. Whether they remain deserving of a similar critique today is a question each of us must answer for ourselves. Certainly they had earned the licking that Koch gave them. He takes accurate aim at "the poetry / Written by the men with their eyes on the myth / And the Missus and the midterms in the *Hudson Review*" and laments, "what is one to do / With the rest of one's day that lies blasted to ruins / All bluely about one, what is one to do?" He has no recourse, it seems. The end lines of this part contain an especially clever twist:

> And supposing one goes to the *Hudson Review*
> With a pack of matches and sets fire to the building?
> One ends up in prison with trial subscriptions
> To the *Partisan, Sewanee* and *Kenyon Review*!

The last section of the poem, part five, is the longest and makes for a rousing conclusion. Koch invokes the title phrase, fresh air, and personifies it as a female art student toward whom he feels both admiring and amorous. He is so worked up at this point that he can't decide whether he and little Miss Fresh Air should "paint the poets" (as so many New York poets painted him and his friends), "Give them a little inspiration," or "be sea air! be noxious! kill them, if you must, but stop their poetry!" As it happens, fresh air leaves, and things take a turn for the worse. Despite the author's best intentions to banish all superfluous references to classical mythology from modern poetry, the myths intrude anyway. Suddenly he's babbling about a gull that becomes a swan that becomes Zeus, Achilles and Helen. He lets out a cry: "One more mistake and I get thrown out of the Modern Poetry Association, help! Why are there no adjectives around?"

The poet appears to be subjected to some kind of forced reeducation, ending with a suggestion that he imitate a horse which is emptying its bowels, as horses sometimes do. He renders all of this in a delicate and roundabout way of course. Koch asks pitifully, "Is there no other way to fertilize minds?"

Just when neither the narrator nor the reader can stand any more, a serving girl enters. She is in fact the art student, fresh air, in a different guise (which, ironically, is exactly what happens in such ancient mythic classics as *The Odyssey*, where the gods are always assuming different forms in their efforts to punish or aid humanity). The poet and his girl are literally walking off into the sunset—or sunrise, it isn't clear—and waving goodbye to the odd ghastly presences that have haunted the poem: "Good luck to you, Strangler!" "Goodbye, manure!" And finally:

> Until tomorrow, then, scum floating on the surface of poetry! goodbye for a moment, refuse that happens to land in poetry's boundaries! adieu, stale eggs teaching imbeciles poetry to bolster your own egos! [. . .]
> Ah, but the scum is deep! Come, let me help you! and soon we pass into the clear blue water [. . .]
> Hello, sea! good morning, sea! hello, clarity and excitement, you great expanse of green—
> O green, beneath which all of them shall drown!

I have read and reread this mighty poem countless times. It never fails to make me laugh, and to rouse me back to my mission. It continues to remind me that it is always the right time for renewal, for a return to first principles, to a primal way of seeing, listening and singing. Great art is not made by committee or groupthink, whether aesthetic or political or even spiritual. No one ever has or ever will workshop or MFA a great poem into being. Only a voice crying in the wilderness can bring true wildness and imagination back into our literature, which is too often oh-so-tame and trying oh-so-hard to pretend to be something else.

NOTE: While I used many resources for this essay and have quoted from some of them, the most helpful book was one I did not have occasion to quote from directly, *The Last Avant-Garde* by David Lehman (Doubleday 1998). For me, this is the most penetrating and insightful book about the New York School poets, and I say that knowing it has lots of worthy competition. If you are at all interested in that movement or Kenneth Koch or "Fresh Air," you owe it to yourself to read this book.

A Villanelle for Kenneth

There is nobody quite like Kenneth Koch,
No one in this world or any other
Having such serious fun with a joke.

If poetry's the egg, he is the yolk.
The nine muses call Kenneth their mother.
There is nobody quite like Kenneth Koch.

His brilliant flame always brings forth some smoke
From critics Kenneth would gladly smother,
Having such serious fun with a joke.

Said he, "Our poets are bankrupt! They're broke!
I'd kill them all if I had my druthers!"
There is nobody quite like Kenneth Koch.

Ashbery, Schuyler, O'Hara and Koch,
The New York School is our Band of Brothers
Having such serious fun with a joke.

Let every frog that dares rhyme feebly croak,
"Kenneth is gone! There won't be another.
There is nobody quite like Kenneth Koch
Having such serious fun with a joke."

HOMER

The Odyssey: Excerpt from Book 22: "Bloodshed"

By Homer
translated by Emily Wilson

Showing initiative, Telemachus
insisted,

       "I refuse to grant these girls
a clean death, since they poured down shame on me
and Mother, when they lay beside the suitors."

At that, he wound a piece of sailor's rope
round the rotunda and round the mighty pillar,
stretched up so high no foot could touch the ground
As doves or thrushes spread their wings to fly
home to their nests, but someone sets a trap—
they crash into a net, a bitter bedtime:
just so the girls, their heads all in a row,
were strung up with the noose around their necks
to make their death an agony. They gasped,
feet twitching for a while, but not for long.

Then the men took Melanthius outside
and with curved bronze cut off of his nose and ears
and ripped away his genitals, to feed
raw to the dogs. Still full of rage, they chopped
his hands and feet off. Then they washed their own
and they went back inside.

Found in Translation: Homer Through the Eyes of Emily Wilson

We can never have too many translations of a great work of literature. There is always the chance, or the hope, that a new version will bring out some crucial aspect of the work that previous versions have missed. We want a new translation to be at the same time more faithful to the original and also more exciting in our own language, as if combining our wife and our mistress into the same being. Once in a lifetime a new translation achieves these goals on such a scale that it flattens the competition and rises to a whole different level, the level of the original work. This is what Emily Wilson has accomplished with her translations of *The Odyssey* and *The Iliad* by Homer. It is impossible to imagine them being equaled, let alone surpassed, any time soon.

"Who is Kurt Luchs," you may ask, "that he dares torment us with his pontifications upon works written in a dead language that he doesn't presume to know?" Well, fair enough. I'll go so far as to forgive that your imaginary question is so laborious and stilted that it sounds as if it was brought over from an even deader language. It's still a fair question. And the answer is, you're right. My knowledge of Ancient Greek is limited to a scene from the Marx Brothers film *Animal Crackers*, where Captain Jeffrey T. Spaulding (Groucho) is dictating a letter to his secretary Horatio Jamison (Zeppo). Groucho criticizes Zeppo's diction, and adds, "You want to brush up on your Greek, Jamison. Well, get a Greek and brush up on him!" It is not known what connection there might be between this classic exchange and the later Cole Porter song "Brush Up Your Shakespeare" from *Kiss Me Kate*.

What I can say is that it is precisely because I have brushed up my Shakespeare, and my Milton, and all the other worthy poets in the English language who have created a centuries-old tradition of blank verse in iambic pentameter, that I do have some ability to judge Wilson's work as poetry in our tongue. Not only do her translations of Homer make these epics sing in a way they never have previously for modern readers, and thus reaffirm Homer's greatness. They also prove that she is among the finest poets of our time. That is not something she would claim for herself. On the contrary, in the last paragraph of her Translator's Note for *The Iliad*, she refers to herself as a "mere translator." Her humility is admirable and exactly the right spirit with which to approach the monumental task she undertook. But it must be said that it takes a great poet to translate a great poem, to recreate it line by line in another language in a way that does it justice, faithful like a wife, exciting like a mistress.

Even if these translations were less than magnificent, these books would be worth having for the introductions, probably the most entertaining and insightful musings on Homer ever penned. Further, she uses the introductions and translator's notes to explain her choices. And here we can see how she avoided the pitfalls of most previous versions.

The originals were written in dactylic hexameter, a line and rhythm that might make perfect sense in Ancient Greek but which sounds like horses galloping or the oom-pah-pah of a tuba in English. For better or worse, the only sensible English equivalent to the prosody of Homer is iambic pentameter. It sounds more like soldiers marching. By adding or subtracting a syllable here and there and occasionally switching up the beat, it can be capable of tremendous variety. Homer's poems were not rhymed, so there is no rationale for a translation to be (sorry, Alexander Pope, your version of *The Odyssey* is a nonstarter for this reason alone).

Blank verse it is then! Not, however, the blank verse of Shakespeare or Milton, wonderful though they are. Wilson takes pains to avoid any trace of archaic diction, unlike, say, the Technicolor biblical epics of the 1950s. The diction in many of those films at least had some point, because it descended in a straight line from the translations in the King James Bible. Such a cliched device would do nothing to bring us any closer to the world of these poems.

And what a strange, incomprehensible world it is for those of us looking back from the twenty-first century. The founders of this nation took many ideas about democracy, the governance of republics and human rights from Ancient Greece and Rome. These poems, however, predate the Greece where the first stirrings of democracy and freedom were felt. In fact, though written in Greek, they predate Greece. Nowhere in them can be found any notion of essential human rights, the equality of women, the errors of racism and nationalism, and the evils of wars of conquest. By the end of *The Iliad* the characters have become deeply aware of the horrible suffering and destruction of war, but they cannot look outside the framework of their time to question the whole enterprise.

War was the means by which talented and ambitious men won honor. It was also the means by which they obtained wealth, through plundering and pillaging those they had defeated, and claiming every kind of trophy, up to and including human beings. That's what Helen was if you'll recall, a trophy. Every kind of theft was legal and even meritorious in warfare. *The Odyssey* contains multiple passages admiring the clever piracy of its protagonist.

The worst evil, from our modern viewpoint, was slavery. In the world of these poems it was ubiquitous. The most striking thing about it is that nobody questions it, least of all the slaves themselves. The slave rebellions of Rome were centuries in the future. When a woman is captured by the enemy in wartime, she knows she'll be enslaved, raped, and kept as a powerless concubine for the rest of her life.

Of course, slavery is far from extinguished even in our time. It is still practiced in Chinese gulags and in parts of the Middle East and Africa, and in a sub rosa form anywhere there is human trafficking. But it is quite peculiar to be immersed in the world of these epics where it is universal and taken for granted.

As readers from a different time with different values and social structures, we should feel alienated from these foreign tales. Yet we do not. Despite the gulf between us and Homer, we share many human feelings, and feelings are the basis of art. We too grow up in families, study, work, worship, fall in love and start families of our own. And when necessary, either to obtain honor or riches, or to defend them, we fight for what we love and believe in, to the death if we must, though most of our battles occur in boardrooms and the marketplace and are not immediately fatal.

Part of Wilson's achievement lies in how she has artfully tuned the English diction of these translations to bring out the same feelings in us as the original poems presumably did in their listeners. It's worth noting, also, that she is the first woman to translate these works in their entirety. For the first time, perhaps, we can be reasonably sure that the misogyny, racism and imperialism that we find in them are the creation of Homer alone and have not been unintentionally enhanced by a biased male translator.

I could go on about her canny and erudite choices and how well they serve Homer, but you can see that for yourself in her introductions and translator's notes. It's time for a look at some of the results. Wilson's personal favorite of the two epics is *The Iliad*, for reasons she explains well. Mine is *The Odyssey*, because it seems to me the more universal, though perhaps it is just a matter of which parts of the human experience Homer focuses on in each poem. For me, anyway, the premise of a long, fraught journey homeward to an uncertain reception resonates more.

I can't hope to cover the entire poem in an essay of this scope. Instead I will look at one of the twenty-four chapters (actually, they're called books). Let's examine some of the highlights of Book 22, "Bloodshed," which is the climax of the narrative. This is where Odysseus, after twenty years of wandering, is back in his own home in Ithaca disguised as a ragged beggar. He finally reveals himself to the suitors that have been hounding his wife Penelope for her hand (thinking her a widow), and slaughters them all with the help of his son Telemachus and some loyal longtime servants (okay, slaves).

The first thing one notices about this book is how aptly it has been titled. "Bloodshed" it's called and bloodshed there is, by the bucketful. Nor is Homer shy about depicting it graphically. His crimson-soaked telling makes *MacBeth* seem like a Sunday school pageant. I'm surprised that Sam Peckinpah and Quentin Tarantino have never filmed a version of this story. Here, for example, is what Odysseus has his men do to Melanthius, the goatherd who helped the suitors plunder the flocks of the household for their nightly feasts as they courted Penelope:

> Then the men took Melanthius outside
> and with curved bronze cut off of his nose and ears
> and ripped away his genitals, to feed
> raw to the dogs. Still full of rage, they chopped
> his hands and feet off. Then they washed their own
> and they went back inside.

Note the alliteration of "curved" and "cut," and also of "ripped," "raw" and "rage." Just enough to make a song of the narrative. The whole translation is like this: simple, subtle and supple. The directness of the brutal episode and its matter-of-fact delivery would make Hemingway proud. Right before this passage, Telemachus dispatches the twelve slave girls who betrayed their mistress and bedded down with the suitors:

> As doves or thrushes spread their wings to fly
> home to their nests, but someone sets a trap—
> they crash into a net, a bitter bedtime:
> just so the girls, their heads all in a row,
> were strung up with the noose around their necks
> to make their death an agony. They gasped,
> feet twitching for a while, but not for long.

Odysseus, Telemachus and a few loyal herdsmen prove enough of a force to annihilate every suitor. But the gods have been involved as well from the beginning of this tale. They have contributed to the hero's suffering and one of them will play a vital role in his victory. Athena, daughter of Zeus, and like Odysseus a master strategist, twice causes the suitors' spears and arrows to miss their marks.

We should pause here to consider how different the religion of the Ancient Greeks shown in these poems is from Christianity as preached, yet how similar to Christianity as practiced. The gods of Mount Olympus are simply humans writ large in both their virtues and vices, with Marvel superpowers added. They are temperamental, fickle, whimsical, and often vicious and cruel and vengeful. We of modern times, who fancy ourselves sophisticated and advanced, feel we would have trouble worshipping and obeying such beings whose moral sense is manifestly inferior to our own. The Judeo-Christian god, by contrast, is all-powerful and all-knowing but also all-loving and all-forgiving. Supplicants to Jehovah are urged to pray to be or become, not to get. The spiritual goal is to be more like him, not to get him to do things for us.

Well, saints like Augustine and Aquinas may live up to these ideals. The rest of us do not. Exactly like the characters of Homer's poems, we beg our god, we try to bribe him with offerings and promises of good behavior, and we implore him to give us what we want, no matter how impure or selfish our motives. Even worse, we subconsciously expect our god to understand this because the Old Testament shows him to be about as high-minded and emotionally stable as Zeus. All this to say, the emotional life and even the spiritual life of Homer's characters is not so far removed from us as it might first appear.

Back to the poem! The only other thing I want to touch on is the running theme of how the travels and travails of Odysseus have aged him and changed him in his twenty-year journey. He expresses much anxiety over the twin dilemmas of how he can conceal his identity when he returns to Ithaca, and then how he can reveal himself convincingly before he exacts his revenge and takes back what is his.

Athena helps him with the first dilemma by using her powers to make Odysseus look even older and more ragged than his journeys have. This allows him to return to Ithaca unrecognized and to infiltrate his own household in the guise of an aged beggar. Athena helps with the second dilemma also, by removing the enchantments of age from Odysseus at critical moments, such as when he wants to be known by Telemachus.

More often, however, Odysseus reveals himself by letting the doubters see and touch the deep scar left in his thigh during his first wild boar hunt as a young man. There is nothing more intimate than a wound. While this wound is physical, it doubles as a symbol of the inner wounding of Odysseus during his unimaginable ordeals, his psychic suffering, his doubts, his fears.

And it has a curious echo in the New Testament account of the resurrection of Christ, when doubting Thomas must touch the wound in Jesus' side to be convinced that he's back. In fact, there is a remarkable parallel between these passages of *The Odyssey* and the inexplicable reactions of Jesus' followers when he reappears among them on several occasions after his crucifixion. It has always struck me as very odd that his disciples, who have been with him constantly for three years, don't seem to know him at all when they see him again. The women do, naturally, because women may see some things more readily than men.

Yet the men remain clueless. Aside from the general dull-wittedness of the disciples, the most obvious explanation is that these unrecognized appearances of the risen Lord are not the risen Lord at all, merely misinterpreted and misremembered after the fact to fit the legend. Still, it is tantalizing to compare them with similar passages in *The Odyssey*, because they both employ one of the oldest religious tropes in existence, that of the trickster god. This too may help us relate to the emotional and spiritual world of Homer, as far removed as we like to think we are from everything else about him.

The Sign of Odysseus

No one seems to recognize him
this ragged old man begging for scraps
in his own house like a feral dog

After twenty years away across the sea
fighting the Trojans to their doom
plundering foreign villages as any pirate would
watching his men be slaughtered
and servicing the pleasure of a goddess
he has returned to a home no longer his
his son not quite a man
his wife not quite a widow
the suitors wasting his substance
coming ever closer to a sanctified rape

Nobody knows him
nobody gives him a second glance
to see what's beneath the grime of decades
how can he announce himself
to a world that has stopped awaiting him

The gods can open the eyes of those he loves
the gods can do anything
and that's lazy writing Homer
much better to share secrets
things that only he would know
yet even that is not enough
an imposter could have heard these things
from his own dying lips
and returned in his place to claim his treasure

TRIBUTARIES

In the end there is but one sure sign
the wound given in his flesh
by the first wild boar he hunted and killed
the wound healed long ago but the scar remains
as personal as a signature
if you want them to know who you really are
show them your wound

LOUISE GLÜCK

Mother and Child

By Louise Glück

We're all dreamers; we don't know who we are.

Some machine made us; machine of the world, the constricting family.
Then back to the world, polished by soft whips.

We dream; we don't remember.

Machine of the family: dark fur, forests of the mother's body.
Machine of the mother: white city inside her.

And before that: earth and water.
Moss between rocks, pieces of leaves and grass.

And before, cells in a great darkness.
And before that, the veiled world.

This is why you were born: to silence me.
Cells of my mother and father, it is your turn
to be pivotal, to be the masterpiece.

I improvised; I never remembered.
Now it's your turn to be driven;
you're the one who demands to know:

Why do I suffer? Why am I ignorant?
Cells in a great darkness. Some machine made us;
it is your turn to address it, to go back asking
what am I for? What am I for?

MATERNAL AND ETERNAL MYSTERIES: THE INTERROGATIONS OF LOUISE GLÜCK

The verse on greeting cards comforts us for half a second because it pretends to give answers and assurances: I love you, god loves us all, there can be peace on earth and goodwill toward men, etc., etc. Actual poetry, if it's any good, offers few assurances and even fewer answers. Like all the arts, it exists to give human utterance to thoughts, feelings and expressions that would never fit on something sold by Hallmark. Like the sciences, it poses the deepest possible questions about the nature of reality and our all-too-brief existence in it. Sometimes the questions are implied rather than stated, but they are always there, again, if the poem is worth reading at all. I'm thinking here, for example, of the implied question that concludes the brilliant Robert Frost sonnet "Design": "If design govern in a thing so small."

Poets are playful and mischievous creatures, the leprechauns of literature if you will, which is why they occasionally tweak us by pretending to ask trivial questions in order to surprise us with a sudden stab to the heart. Could there be any question less consequential than the one asked by T. S. Eliot in "The Love Song of J. Alfred Prufrock," "Do I dare to eat a peach?" In the context of the poem, however, the question becomes devastating and heart-breaking. It continues to reverberate and even found a place in popular culture in the title of the Allman Brothers album *Eat a Peach* from 1972.

The Louise Glück poem we're looking at here, "Mother and Child," consists almost entirely of questions. It starts with implicit questions and ends with quite explicit ones. This movement provides most of the form in this succinct twenty-line piece of free verse. The rest comes from the poet's canny use of reiteration and what might be called variations on a theme. There are few overt poetics here, no rhyme, not even internal rhyme, and very little alliteration or assonance. It is stripped to the bone, the literary equivalent of Duchamp's artwork "The Bride Stripped Bare by Her Bachelors, Even" (aka "The Large Glass"), as laconic as a poem can be short of becoming pure silence. In other words, it is a typical Louise Glück poem, and all the better for it.

The title "Mother and Child" seems deliberately ironic, having been used by countless painters good and bad. She could have called it "Madonna and Child," but why drag Lourdes into it? The poor kid has enough to deal with. We know that Glück's poetry generally moves from the autobiographical to the universal. We also know that the most important relationships in her life were with her mother and her younger sister, territory covered in the final book published in her lifetime, her first and only fiction *Marigold and Rose* (2022).

"Mother and Child" is from her ninth book, *The Seven Ages* (2001). Many of the poems in this collection ponder her mortality and this one does too. More than the others, though, this poem seeks to peer back through time to a number of essential beginnings: the beginning of her life and consciousness, and by extension the beginning of all human life and consciousness. The twenty lines of the poem are broken into nine stanzas. The stanzas in the first half—which I take to be the first six—are all one or two lines long. Here are the first two:

> We're all dreamers; we don't know who we are.
>
> Some machine made us, machine of the world, the constricting family.
> Then back to the world, polished by soft whips.

The first stanza implies that we can't know ourselves until we awaken from our dream state. The dream state is where we all begin and many of us never leave it, never achieve consciousness or self-awareness. There is such a thing as guided dreaming, where you learn how to direct your dreams and how to remain aware, within the dream, that you are dreaming. That's obviously not what Glück is talking about here.

"Some machine made us," she begins in the second stanza. By immediately refining this down to "machine of the world," she seems to be referring to what evolutionist Richard Dawkins calls "the blind watchmaker." Where is god or the possibility of god in all this? Napoleon asked French mathematician Pierre-Simon Laplace the same question, to which Laplace famously replied, "Sir, I have no need of that hypothesis."

She further refines the image down to "the constricting family," one of her favorite subjects. Every family is its own kind of machine, or its own system. As economist F. A. Hayek might have said in another context, each family is "the result of human action but not of human design." (he was talking about the self-organizing aspects of the market). Our parents pass on to us the haphazard genetic inheritance they received from their parents, along with whatever random sense or nonsense or absolute madness reigned in their families. And so we are shaped.

Now comes one of her best lines: "Then back to the world, polished by soft whips." What a haunting phrase! It isn't absolutely clear whether it's the family or the world that provides the soft whips, which gives it a rich ambiguity, but the structure of the stanza and the line implies the latter. It sounds as if in Glück's family, as in mine, the whips were seldom soft. Also, I'm guessing in her case the whips were metaphorical, not literal as they were for many of us.

The single line of stanza three provides a reiteration of and a variation on stanza one, except that instead of not knowing who we are, there is the broader statement "we don't remember." Don't remember what? Presumably anything.

Stanzas four through six consist of two lines each. They begin to move the poem forward after the provocative scene-setting of the opening. The "Machine of the world" is further refined to "Machine of the mother," and refers mysteriously to the "white city inside her." What is that? I have no idea. It's an evocative phrase but I don't know what it's evoking. Stanza five turns the clock back further to a time when there were no humans or animals of any kind, only "earth and water" with moss, leaves and grass. There is one final leap back backward in stanza six, where she speaks of ". . .cells in a great darkness. / And before that, the veiled world." Of course the world is veiled in the sense that the earliest fossil record is so scant and difficult to interpret after four billion years. However, I think this is also where the poem turns, where metaphysical mystery gets added to scientific mystery. The world is veiled and the meaning of it even more so.

The last half of the poem is comprised of stanzas seven through nine. Stanzas seven and eight have three lines each, more than any others so far, and the poem concludes with the almost fulsome four lines of stanza nine. One way of looking at this structure is that Glück paints a strange, disturbing picture in the first half, and spends the second half commenting on it and interrogating it with increasing urgency as her anguished questions accumulate.

Stanza seven starts with a bang (apologies to Ethan Siegel): "That is why you were born: to silence me." After all the metaphor and mystery of the previous stanzas, this straightforward, utterly assured declaration is a bit shocking. Some mystery remains, though. Is she talking about her own son, her only child Noah, to whom the book in which the poem appears is partly dedicated? Or is she taking her mother's voice and referring to herself? As best as I can figure, she means it both ways. The stanza continues: "Cells of my mother and father, it is your turn / to be pivotal, to be the masterpiece." Again, the same cells are in her and in her son. There is a great matrilineal chain of being, and not simply with the mitochondrial DNA, but with the mother who nurtures and constricts and polishes with soft whips.

After a brief reiteration of and a variation on stanzas one and three—"I improvised, I never remembered"—the poem races to a frantic ending:

> Now it is your turn to be driven;
> you're the one who demands to know:
>
> Why do I suffer? Why am I ignorant?
> Cells in a great darkness. Some machine made us;
> it is your turn to address it, to go back asking
> what am I for? What am I for?

That last question is as old as humanity and as current as the 2024 Oscar-winning song by Billie Eilish from the movie *Barbie*, "What Was I Made For?". Plaintively, piteously—but also, as she says, driven—she must repeat the question. The reiteration underscores the sorrowful fact that she got no answer the first time. If she had, she might also be able to answer the questions that begin the final stanza: "Why do I suffer? Why am I ignorant?" Wiser people than myself have long postulated that suffering is essential to understanding and embracing our purposes as humans on planet earth. Without it, how can we possibly have empathy? How can we comprehend and begin to correct our potential for harm as individuals and as a species? How, to return to one of this poem's central metaphors, can we ever hope to step out of the machine and achieve genuine consciousness?

As for being ignorant, yes, we are born that way. Many of us then spend the better part of our life's energy striving to remain that way, engaging in various forms of denial. We eat something called "food" that does not nourish. We take in something called "news" that, these days, seldom contains a single verified fact, only hate, outrage and contempt aimed at furthering a particular ideology or party. When we do engage with our emotions, we send and receive greeting cards, skimming the surface of our feelings, carefully avoiding the depths.

One reason I have always treasured the work of Louise Glück, particularly in poems like "Mother and Child," is that she "demands to know." She asks the hard questions. She kept on asking them right up to the end. And unlike our so-called leaders, she doesn't pretend to have the answers when she doesn't. As Covid should have taught us, ignorance is not the worst thing that can happen to us. It's curable, and both art and science are part of the cure. There is nothing worse than the pretense of knowledge, the delusion of competence. Both have killed or injured so many of us these past few years.

I love Glück because she acknowledges that ignorance is our starting point yet she refuses to let it be our end point. If you want cheap sentiment and superficial cuteness, go to Hallmark. If you seek truth and wisdom, go to the hard cold beauty of poems like this, which I believe compares favorably with the later work of Yeats. Go to Glück.

To My Chinese Daughters

We didn't make you
your adoptive mother and I
but you made us

Your Chinese mothers made you
and either didn't love you enough
to keep you

fearful of the one child law
or loved you so much they had
to keep you alive

even if it meant hiding their pregnancies
at great personal risk and sacrifice
giving birth in secret (I prefer that version)

hidden in a city apartment
or a hut in the countryside
muffling their cries through the night

no doctors no nurses no morphine
then suddenly there were two cries
in the room

and there you were each of you
a fresh new living soul
and a problem to be solved

Having loved you all the way to birth
the limit of human endurance
in the China of that day

the question was where to drop you
where you would survive a few hours
until you were discovered

and sent to one of the country's
eight hundred orphanages
filled with millions of baby girls

plus a few boys with harelips
Nora your mother left you
at a hospital construction site in Xian City

home of the buried ceramic warriors
Jia they found you in a farmer's field
in Guangxi in the south

Each of you made it through months
in places where starvation and neglect
killed up to ninety percent of the children

and then you came to us
neither of us fully human
unfit to be married

let alone to each other
lost in every way a human can be lost
not knowing who we were

or why we were together
or what we were for
until they put you in our arms

ROBERT BLY

Hunting Pheasants in a Cornfield

By Robert Bly

I

What is so strange about a tree alone in an open field?
It is a willow tree. I walk around and around it.
The body is strangely torn, and cannot leave it.
At last I sit down beneath it.

II

It is a willow tree alone in acres of dry corn.
Its leaves are scattered around its trunk, and around me,
Brown now, and speckled with delicate black,
Only the cornstalks now can make a noise.

III

The sun is cold, burning through the frosty distances of space.
The weeds are frozen to death long ago.
Why then do I love to watch
The sun moving on the chill skin of the branches?

IV

The mind has shed leaves alone for years.
It stands apart with small creatures near its roots.
I am happy in this ancient place,
A spot easily caught sight of above the corn,
If I were a young animal ready to turn home at dusk.

Hunting Everything but Pheasants with Robert Bly

In some ways, the place of Robert Bly in our literature during his heyday can be compared to that of Ezra Pound during his. Pound was the leader and the center of the revolution in American and English poetry that took place in the early decades of the last century. The circumstances were unique and unlikely to ever be repeated. In any case, they haven't been. The number of poets and literary journals that mattered was small, and he knew them all. Even the ones who despised him—and there were more than a few, as noted by Robert Frost, who referred to Pound's "gentle art of making enemies"— were influenced by him, almost against their will, such was the power of his personality and his passion for poetry. Though Yeats was twenty years his senior, Pound paradoxically mentored him into the new age and was certainly a key influence on his later and best work. Pound could befriend both T. S. Eliot and William Carlos Williams, living symbols of the clash between formalism and free verse who didn't like or understand each other (the best book about that is *Three on the Tower* by Louis Simpson). As the facsimile edition of "The Waste Land" made plain, it was Pound who gave that famous poem its final form.

Robert Bly also led a revolution in our poetry several generations later, though by then the world of poetry was so fragmented that no one figure, not even Bly, could command the influence once wielded by Pound. By the time Bly came on the scene in the 1950s, the poetry revolution of the early twentieth century had become the establishment. Large swathes of the literary scene consisted of poets trying to out-Eliot Eliot, such as Robert Lowell, or to out-Auden Auden, such as Howard Nemerov. The leading magazines had become dull and predictable, not unlike today. Clearly, another revolution was needed.

Several were already in motion, in fact. While the permanent worth of some of the Beatniks' work will continue to be debated (and I'm a bit of a doubter myself, as I doubt almost everything), there's no denying they brought poetry back into popular culture and public consciousness. They made live poetry readings a vogue again. They affiliated themselves with the most intelligent popular music of the time, jazz. And finally, they made it acceptable to write political poems again, as it had not been since the 1930s. That's all in their favor.

At the same time, a very different revolution was being led by the New York school of poets, with John Ashbery, Kenneth Koch, Frank O'Hara and James Schuyler at the fore. They had in common with the Beats a sense of humor. Where the Beats tended to act the clown in public, or perhaps more fairly to be seen as jesters, the New York poets were wits and proudly sophisticated and international in their tastes. Both groups were inveterate pranksters. Even James Dickey, who never liked any Beat poet ever, enjoyed the sharp yet humane humor of Ginsberg.

The thing is, these divisions were almost total on the literary as well as the personal level. These groups did not mix much. They tended to share a mutual contempt for each other and the establishment. Each had their own magazines and anthologies, and when they deigned to review the work outside their own cliques they would spit venom like cobras. How funny it all seems now. And how different from today, when there are no schools of poetry worthy of the name, not even to ridicule, and practically nobody dares give a book a bad review. Poetry may still be half-alive (again, I am dubious), but criticism is deader than the Lindbergh baby.

But to return to Mr. Bly. The third poetic revolution, the one he led, was a rebellion against the stuffy, academic, denatured verse that dominated the establishment poets of the fifties. Against all odds, some of these poets still managed to write good poems. Lowell may be a waste of space, for example, but Nemerov is actually well worth reading. Overall, however, the Beats, the New York poets and the less definable school led by Bly had a point. Poetry had in some essential way gone off the rails. Or maybe the problem was the opposite: poetry had become too tame and timidly stayed in its own little lane, not greatly affected by or affecting anything else. This too sounds very similar to our current situation.

Bly recognized the problem and sought to correct it in several ways. He understood that formalism had been exhausted and ruined as a technique, at least for the moment, for most poets, so he pushed for a free verse revolution. The Beats were in complete agreement of course, the New York poets not so much. Especially Koch, who showed that a dead formalism can be revived at any time by infusing it with life, love and laughter.

Secondly, Bly grasped that American poets needed to look for inspiration and models outside of their immediate past and their country's borders. For him and many others in his circle, this mostly meant digging into the work of the great Hispanic poets such as Lorca, Neruda, Machado, Jimenez, Borges, Hernandez, Vallejo, Mistral, etc. Meanwhile the New York poets looked mainly to the French, and the Beats, apart from understandably idolizing Whitman, looked outside of literature altogether.

Finally, Bly and his fellow travelers wanted to focus less on verbal pyrotechnics and more on what he called the "subjective image" (others called it the "deep image"), the mysterious, dreamlike, nonreducible heart of the poem. Some of his leading fellow travelers, not necessarily always in agreement with his program or his poetics, included James Wright, W. S. Merwin, Louis Simpson and John Logan, among others. Notice that it was a boy's club. Many things were back then. One of the positive changes about the current poetry scene is that for the first time ever, most of the best poets are women, of which Ada Limon is an excellent exemplar.

Both Bly and Logan edited magazines, two of the most significant and useful of their time. Bly started the *Fifties*, which became the *Sixties* and then the *Seventies*. It never got to the *Eighties*, but by then his work of reconstruction was done. Logan helmed *Choice*, which, among other things, published Bly's groundbreaking and controversial essay, "A Wrong Turning in American Poetry." We are badly in need of a sequel to that. I could write it myself, but I won't, because what happened to Bly after he wrote his manifesto—a successful revolution—is not what would happen to me. Nothing would change except that I would be canceled and doxed and never heard from again, my career in literature (or at least in poetry) over forever. The sad truth is that I kind of want to get somewhere in this business before they send me to the (hopefully metaphorical) guillotine. Yes, I am a moral and intellectual coward. I'm not proud of it, but there it is.

Well, that's enough of a preamble for any poetic career and any poem! The Bly poem under discussion today is "Hunting Pheasants in a Cornfield," from his first full-length collection *Silence in the Snowy Fields* (Wesleyan 1962), issued when he was thirty-six. He had waited a while to publish. In that sense most of his contemporaries were way ahead of him, especially

Merwin, a year younger than him, who already had four books under his belt and the fifth, his own groundbreaker *The Moving Target*, coming in 1963. Bly's delay was intentional, however. He felt that a poet shouldn't put out a book until he was at least thirty and knew who he (or she) was. He didn't wait quite as long as one of his heroes, Wallace Stevens, whose first volume *Harmonium* came in 1923 when he was forty-four. Just for comparison, ponder the fact that by the time Keats was forty-four he had been dead for eighteen years.

For Bly, the wait was worth it. This is a man who knows what he knows. *Silence in the Snowy Fields* feels confident and assured without being arrogant, fresh without straining for novelty. The poems are all short, none of them more than a page. Half a dozen of them are only five lines or less. At seventeen lines, "Hunting Pheasants in a Cornfield" is one of the longer poems here. It is divided into four numbered stanzas, the first three consisting of four lines each and the last one containing five.

The first thing to notice about it is that the pheasants appear only in the title, and by implication in the last line. In other words, the title tells us what brought him to the cornfield. The poem tells us what he found there, starting in stanza one:

> What is so strange about a tree alone in an open field?
> It is a willow tree. I walk around and around it.
> The body is strangely torn, and cannot leave it.
> At last I sit down beneath it.

He thought he was hunting pheasants, yet it's almost as if the tree was hunting him. He has been completely captured by it. As John Lennon says in the song "Beautiful Boy," "Life is what happens when we're busy making other plans." At this point the poet is not even fully conscious of what is happening. It's his body that is "strangely torn," not his mind. Although he doesn't mention what he's wearing or carrying, the season and the activity mean he must have on an overcoat and be holding a shotgun. One of the subtlest effects of the poem is how the tree disarms him without it ever being openly acknowledged that he is armed (a man sitting like Buddha beneath a willow tree is not thinking about his shotgun). And isn't this what all great art does? It takes us by surprise, peels back our protections and takes us out of ourselves and whatever we thought we were doing.

Stanza two pays more attention to specifics about the tree, showing that the poet's mind has become engaged with the mysterious attraction. He notes that the willow is totally isolated in "acres of dry corn." The second line plays a key role, as it will have a sequel in the final stanza: "Its leaves are scattered around its trunk, and around me." Bly has become one with the tree, if only in his imagination, in order to find out what's going on. Ever the carefully observant naturalist, he sees that the tree's fallen brown leaves are "speckled with delicate black." Little dots of death, perhaps? When he says in the last line of the stanza, "Only the cornstalks now can make a noise", he tells us that the wind blows through the remains of the corn and reminds us that the tree is not only alone but silent. Just as he is.

Suddenly in stanza three he makes one of those characteristic Robert Bly leaps (recall that he edited an anthology called *Leaping Poetry*), speaking of the cold winter sun "burning through the frosty distances of space." I believe this is his way of tying the tree's aloneness and his own to the loneliness of planet Earth. The word "death," which has been hovering at the fringes of the poem, gets said out loud for the first and only time when he mentions the dead frozen weeds in line two of this stanza. The conclusion of stanza three puts these things together to give a particular spin to his fascination with the tree: "Why then do I love to watch / The sun moving on the chill skin of the branches?" Why indeed? The sun cannot warm during this frozen hunting season. But it can still illuminate, like the awakened mind. And now we are ready for stanza four:

> The mind has shed leaves alone for years.
> It stands apart with small creatures near its roots.
> I am happy in this ancient place,
> A spot easily caught sight of above the corn,
> If I were a young animal ready to turn home at dusk.

With the first line of this stanza the implicit identification of the poet with the tree has finally been made explicit. The mind "stands apart," as all minds must, though ironically it can only think by means of likenesses; for instance, how it is like a tree, or the sun. It is meaningful that this poem falls in the first section of the book, which is called "Eleven Poems of Solitude" (fyi, the other two sections are called "Awakening" and "Silence on the Roads"). Why is it worth mentioning that the tree in the cornfield is an "ancient place"? And why should it make him happy? Not everything in a poem needs a reason to exist other than beauty and the joy it gives. But I think this is partly his indirect way of letting us know this is a massive willow, a very old tree that spreads both up and out. It's a landmark in the physical world as is his encounter with it in his mind and memory.

The last line of the stanza, and the poem, seems to bring us back to the pheasants that Bly thought he was hunting at the beginning, calling the place of the tree "A spot easily caught sight of above the corn, / If I were a young animal ready to turn home at dusk." Now, nobody goes pheasant hunting at dusk, not if they want to avoid an awkward Dick Cheney moment with the shotgun. In his quiet, oblique way, Bly is giving us an idea of how long he's been sitting under that tree like a Zen apprentice. He would've gone hunting no later than the afternoon, which means it's been hours at least. I find it interesting that he no longer mentions the pheasants by name, as if they aren't on his hit list anymore. And they aren't, because he now identifies with them too. He refers instead to a generic "young animal." In a way, this underscores the feeling the poem leaves us with, of the oneness of all life.

Parting note to young poets, or any poets young at heart: they tell you there are rules for writing, like "avoid the passive voice" and "always be specific." But in truth there are no rules except the tacit rules of intelligence and taste and instinct for what is right in the moment and right for the poem, which often demand that we break the so-called rules. If Bly had listened to the self-appointed rule-makers instead of his own inner spirit, he never could have created this marvelous poem. He never would have set out to hunt pheasants and ended up hunting enlightenment under a bare willow.

The Boulder

The boulder was not magnetic and yet
it drew us to the creek bed
where it sat beside the dark waters
while we sat on it and looked and listened

I say the waters were dark but really
they were clear the darkness
was in the moss rippling beneath them
as if to the tinkling gurgling music rushing past

The granite stone was more than a stool
for beings who did not exist when it was born
it was a gallery with a single exhibit
revealing just how much beauty could be wrought

by pure randomness with no visible artist
the quartz and feldspar flecked with mica
shining even in the shade of the giant cottonwood
inviting eyes and fingers to explore

or simply to rest silently soaking it in
This was the place we came to when our father
tired of hitting us and we slunk away
to be alone or alone together

and to be soothed by the sound of the waters
and the sure presence of the boulder
something older and stronger than us
with no desire to harm us

Occasionally the glint of the mica
would be answered by the flashing scales
of a bluegill swimming furiously against the current
so much energy spent to remain in one place

yes what I'm saying is he was one of us
perhaps also drawn by the boulder's mysterious power
it never would have occurred to us
to try to capture or kill him

There were other places to pause
fallen branches and the chain-sawed stump
of another cottonwood but still the glittering
boulder was always the only choice

and how strange that I should be there right now
though it no longer exists except far down inside me
which may be how what disappears
lives on and the dark waters keep flowing flowing

CHARLES SIMIC

Evening [first version]

By Charles Simic

The snail gives off stillness.
The weed is blessed.
At the end of a long day
The man finds joy, the water peace.

Let all be simple. Let all stand still
Without a final direction.
That which brings you into the world
To take you away at death
Is one and the same;
The shadow long and pointy
Is its church.

At night some understand what the grass says.
The grass knows a word or two.
It is not much. It repeats the same word
Again and again, but not too loudly . . .
The grass is certain of tomorrow.

LISTENING TO THE GRASS AND TO CHARLES SIMIC

We often hear someone described as "a citizen of the world," a silly, empty phrase that usually seems to refer to a person who can afford to jet all over the place without any particular purpose. But in the case of Charles Simic it is the literal truth. Born in Belgrade, Yugoslavia in 1938, he and his Serbian family were among the millions displaced by World War II. They suffered hunger, physical danger, oppression, and the no less severe psychic oppression of being without a real home for years on end. This traumatic formative experience must surely be at the heart of the sense of strangeness and permanent dislocation so central to his poetry.

By 1954 their situation had become dire enough that they immigrated to the United States when Charles was sixteen (his father had come over first, followed by Charles, his mother and his brother). After a year in New York City they relocated to Oak Park, Illinois. He finished high school there and several years later was drafted into the U.S. Army, ironically becoming one of the soldiers who had made his early life so miserable and unsettled. Afterwards he was drawn back to New York and graduated from NYU in 1966.

He had already been writing poems for years, quite excellent poems that were not in the least tentative or immature. He had been forced to grow up quickly, almost at gunpoint. Perhaps because of this he appeared to arrive on the American literary scene fully formed. You could say that his further development as a poet did not involve any significant changes in outlook or approach, only a never-ending quest for greater concision and evocativeness. Has any other writer done so well with English as a second language except for Vladimir Nabokov? I don't think so.

Although Simic's first full-length collection *Dismantling the Silence* would not arrive until 1971, he had already published two chapbooks with *Kayak*, at the time one of the half-dozen most important literary magazines and small presses in the country. His first chapbook *What the Grass*

Says (1967) is as good as anything he ever wrote. With another writer this might be a way of saying that his later work failed to live up to the early promise. With Simic it is simply an acknowledgement of how great he was right from the beginning. According to AbeBooks, a copy of this rare treasure will cost you anywhere from $75 to $505, and let me tell you, it's worth every penny.

The title of *What the Grass Says* comes from a line in the poem we'll be looking at here, called "Evening." This free verse poem is outwardly simple and direct, like most Simic poems. In this original form it consists of three stanzas, the first containing four lines, the second containing seven lines, and the third containing five lines. Later, as we shall see, he cut the last line before including the poem in *Dismantling the Silence*. Here's the first stanza:

> The snail gives off stillness.
> The weed is blessed.
> At the end of a long day
> The man finds joy, the water peace.

There's a lot to unpack here, even at this early stage. The first two sentences are so short that, at two lines, the third sentence almost feels like an epic. It would be easy to say, wait a minute, Mr. Poet, and start questioning things. Isn't the snail always giving off stillness? In what sense can a weed be described as "blessed"? To do so, however, would be unseemly and also beside the point. He's clearly setting the scene here and establishing the mood.

Yes, the snail is always giving off stillness. The little hermaphrodites can sleep for up to three days. But maybe the poet didn't notice the stillness until evening came. The weed could be called blessed in several ways. First of all, for surviving another day without being mowed down (could this also be one reason the man "finds joy"?). And secondly, for merely being part of the idyllic tableau despite its lowly status as an unwanted plant (again, I feel there is an intentional if unstated parallel to the human). Joy can be found in many ways. There is the honest joy of work completed, implied by the "long day." And also the joy of setting aside mundane concerns to enter into the spirit of a special moment at day's end, like the water that has found "peace," presumably because the wind has died down and it is no longer rippling.

The second stanza starts by seeming to reinforce the quiet pastoral feelings of the first stanza. It calls for everything to be "simple" and "still." But then it also calls for everything to be "Without a final direction." Why the sudden note of uncertainty? Well, things are about to get darker rather quickly:

> That which brings you into the world
> To take you away at death
> Is one and the same;
> The shadow long and pointy
> Is its church.

What else does evening bring besides stillness and peace? Lengthening shadows. And these inevitably turn the mind toward the great mysteries of life and death and whether there is anyone or anything behind it all. In other words, the meaning of it all. Only the poem is much more nimble than my prose. It doesn't present the shadow as an overt symbol of anything but rather as a thing-in-itself that happens to embody these resonances. Because that's what humans are, that's what we do. We aren't snails or weeds or even water (at least, not more than sixty percent).

The third and final stanza offers yet another turn that, to my mind, synthesizes the feelings of the first two stanzas. It integrates the quiet stillness with the shadow:

> At night some understand what the grass says.
> The grass knows a word or two.
> It is not much. It repeats the same word
> Again and again, but not too loudly . . .
> The grass is certain of tomorrow.

The idea that nature continually speaks to us is something that science, indigenous cultures and ancient wisdom have in common, though from very different viewpoints. The image of the grass having a simple call, like a bird, is straightforward, charming and distinctly inventive. Which is to say, typical Simic.

It does raise a question, however. In the first stanza the overall stillness and the peace that the water finds suggest that the wind is not blowing.

The breeze, if there was any during the day, has subsided. So, is what the grass says a sound, like the sound the wind makes blowing through a field? Or is it another silence? It could be either. Or both. Sometimes the wind picks up again in the evening as a result of the temperature change. Sorry, I'm not purposefully trying to be too literal here. That's not the best way to approach any poetry, especially Simic's. I simply wish to understand how he created this wonderful poem and how it works its magic on us. Contemplating this poem makes me think of that marvelous Robert Frost couplet, "The Secret Sits": "We dance round in a ring and suppose, / But the Secret sits in the middle and knows."

I'm all right with letting questions remain questions and ambiguities remain ambiguities. One thing I do know is that the original last line is a clunker, an awkward bit of tacked-on anthropomorphism that adds nothing and subtracts a good deal of the mystery. I can hardly believe the line made it into the chapbook that took its title from the poem. Simic was dead right to cut the line when the poem was reprinted in *Dismantling the Silence*.

The business of revising one's work after it has already been published in a book can nonetheless be tricky, as another example from Simic shows. I'm talking about the title poem from *Dismantling the Silence*, which first appeared in his second *Kayak* chapbook *Somewhere Among Us a Stone Is Taking Notes* (1969). When he put it into his first full-length collection it was unchanged. By the time of *Selected Early Poems* (1999) he had lost faith in the ending and tried to fix it. As of course it was absolutely his right to do. Yet in my humble opinion he mucked it up horribly. Thanks to the internet and Kindle and used bookstores we will always have the first version to look at so we can make up our minds. At the end of a long day, that is what brings this man joy.

Mr. Monotonous

He only has two songs, the black-capped chickadee,
more than, say, Debbie Boone or Vanilla Ice,
but still, not much of a musical storehouse.

He takes his name from the five-note cry
chick-a-dee-dee-dee
which makes him sound
like a tiny high-pitched flying Sinatra
in a Beatnik beret.

This time of year, though, they're nesting
and all he seems to have in him
is the little two-note tune
fee-bee
the first note up, the second one down,
over and over,
and that's when I call him Mr. Monotonous.

All right, we get it, you have eggs,
you don't want them to be stolen,
and you're proud you can still
get the missus with child.
Get over yourself, go eat a seed
or an insect and try to have a vocabulary
larger than that of a Chicago alderman.

I hate to tell you, Mr. Monotonous,
but the mourning dove has a song
every bit as limited as yours
only much more beautiful.

She is singing now too
and it's the strangest thing,
something no one intended
and I know you have nothing to do
with each other, yet somehow
you sound so much better together.

JAMES TATE

Poem to Some of My Recent Poems

By James Tate

My beloved little billiard balls,
my polite mongrels, edible patriotic plums,
you owe your beauty to your mother, who
resembled a cylindrical corned beef
with all the trimmings, may God rest
her forsaken soul, for it is all of us
she forsook; and I shall never forget
her sputtering embers, and then the little mound.
Yes, my little rum runners, she had defective
tear ducts and could weep only iced tea.
She had petticoats beneath her eyelids.
And in her last years she found ball bearings
in her beehive puddings, she swore allegiance
to Abyssinia. What should I have done?
I played the piano and scrambled eggs.
I had to navigate carefully around her brain's
avalanche lest even a decent finale be forfeited.
And her beauty still evermore. You see,
as she was dying, I led each of you to her side,
one by one she scorched you with her radiance.
And she is ever with us in our acetylene leisure.
But you are beautiful, and I, a slave to a heap of cinders.

JAMES TATE AND THE SAVING GRACE OF POETIC NARRATIVE

James Tate died in 2015 at the age of seventy-one, after a lifetime devoted to poetry and having won just about every major award, starting with the Yale Younger Series of Poets Award in 1967 when he was only 23, and including a Pulitzer Prize and a National Book Award, among many others. By any measure his career was a huge success, not least in his influence on succeeding generations of poets.

Certainly he has been a key figure in my life as a writer. Few poets have challenged my fundamental notions of what poetry is or can be more than Tate. I have had countless one-sided arguments with him because, it must be said, he infuriates as often as he delights. Since his death I have increasingly found myself reflecting on his example, and when stuck in a poetic corner I sometimes ask myself, "What would Tate do?" knowing that, as like as not, it would be something that would perplex or annoy me.

Whole books have been and will be written about him, I'm sure. My purpose here is to look at a few key aspects of his work, and the light they may shed for the rest of us on the process and goals of writing poetry. In particular I want to examine his lifelong urge toward the outer edges of surrealism and dream logic, and how in the end he found a way to tether that urge with his discovery of the power of narrative, and in the twilight of his career produced what I believe is some of his very best work in the form of transcendental prose poems. Once he started writing them, he never looked back, never returned to his previous free verse, although there remains a good deal of overlap between the two.

According to my thoroughly subjective and personal evaluation, Tate's work can be divided roughly into thirds. One-third of his poems are nonsensical tripe, little more than random gibberish, a lot like early- to middle-period John Ashbery in such poems as, say, "Leaving the Atocha Station" (feel free to kick me in the head if that is one of your favorites by Ashbery). Another third of Tate's poems are failures of one kind or another, but interesting failures with bits of brilliance embedded in them. The remaining third are among the finest poems of our time. What's more, they are fine in ways that are nearly unique to Tate. No one else could have written them. No one else could have shown us this hallucinatory yet recognizable take on the world.

Did he know which of his poems worked and which didn't? Apparently not, because he published all of them. Perhaps a more interesting question is, did he have to write all of the senseless and failed poems in order to write the really good ones, which are not all that different in approach, only in effect?

An example of the first kind of Tate poem, the meaningless kind, is the final poem from a numbered cycle of twenty with the overall title of "Absences," which is also the title of his third full-length collection from 1972. It begins:

> Toto, I don't think we're in Kansas.
> The orange glow of an erased creature
> murdered in comfort by mama's ax
> flies into the organ.

Somewhere around the middle of the poem there is this:

> And eleven elves drop dead
> in the basin of gold trousers.

And it ends like this:

> Nearing an island,
> I forget to wave. It is too beautiful
> to excite me with the idea
> of accessibility.

I won't try your patience any further by pretending to analyze this one. Obviously it defies analysis. The opening could be seen as an oblique warning that we're about to enter uncharted waters, and the ending sort of ties up that idea. But nothing in between makes any kind of sense whatsoever. There is simply the empty feeling of arbitrary words and images rubbing up against each other without adding up to anything. With the exception of the final two sentences, you could rearrange the lines in this poem in any order and it would have the same impact, or lack of impact. That is never a good sign.

Tate wrote many poems like this, around the same time as Bill Knott was also experimenting with extreme surrealism (or aurealism as he quirkily called it), and the same time as Thomas Lux was deciding that, for him anyway, surrealism was a dead end. Knott and Lux found their own ways forward out of the surrealistic swamp. For Knott, it was an intensely idiosyncratic formalism overlaid with wit and savage satire. For Lux, it was a realism rooted in a very generous and nuanced sense of reality, almost Shakespearean in scope. For Tate, as we shall see, it was learning how to use narrative. It's worth noting that the three poets were mutual friends and occasional collaborators. Lux edited Knott's posthumous volume, *I Am Flying into Myself: Selected Poems, 1960–2014*, and Tate and Knott co-wrote a little-known verse collection called *Are You Ready Mary Baker Eddy???* as well as the experimental novel *Lucky Darryl* (good luck finding either of those!).

I should pause here to note that I am not denying the legitimacy of surrealism as a literary technique. I admire its expert use by others and often use it myself, and have even had a chapbook published by SurVision Books, a surrealist house in Dublin, Ireland. What I'm saying is that surrealism by itself did not prove to be a sustainable technique for three of the best American poets born in the forties. I also find it interesting that John Ashbery, a poet-mentor admired by all three of them, also ended up adopting a much more direct and clear style in his later work. Go figure.

I don't think we have room here to deal with Tate's interesting failures, and why they're failed but interesting, so let's skip straight ahead to the best stuff. In his last book before he switched to writing prose poems exclusively, 1997's *Shroud of the Gnome*, he began to introduce more sustained, coherent narrative into his work. We are storytelling creatures after all. It's in our DNA. As a result almost any statement, no matter how bizarre, can take on an air of normalcy and plausibility when told as a story. It's a clever way for a poet to smuggle in odd, dreamlike elements and incorporate them into a meaningful whole. The title poem is an excellent example. It opens in mid-scene like this:

And what amazes me is that none of our modern inventions
surprise or interest him, even a little. I tell him
it is time he got his booster shots, but then
I realize I have no power over him whatsoever.

There follows a funny and seemingly unrelated vignette about the narrator trying to pick up a registered nurse at a lunch counter. Then suddenly he is in an alley, surrounded by "piles of outcast citizenry and burning barrels / of waste and rot, the plump rats darting freely." And at the conclusion (spoiler alert!) he does find the shroud of the gnome:

And now, rejuvenated by the wind, the shroud moves forward,
hesitates, dances sideways, brushes my foot as if for a kiss,
and flies upward, whistling a little-known ballad
about the pitiful, raw etiquette of the underworld.

The poem moves nimbly from humor to a dreamy strangeness (though not quite surrealism), from the mundane to the profound, and in the end is rather heartbreaking. The interlude with the nurse at the lunch counter might seem an irrelevant or distracting bit of comedy at first, but then it segues directly into the "piles of outcast citizenry," and we realize that the narrator, as well as his "lost friend" the gnome, is equally unable to connect with someone outside of his immediate circle and experience, locked into a loneliness as ancient as humanity and as modern as any industrialized city.

We could get into a technical discussion about why I describe this as a prose poem, even though it is not broken into paragraphs and the text doesn't wrap arbitrarily on the right. But I'd rather not. I got into just such a discussion with an editor recently and it didn't lead anywhere useful. Suffice it to say that the long lines, the lack of any metrical or syllabic pattern to the lines, and the recurrent prose-like enjambment are, for me, signs of a prose poem. In any case, Tate himself describes his later work as prose poetry, and that's good enough for me. Allowing authors the grace to self-define seems the most fruitful course.

After *Shroud of the Gnome*, which in retrospect is clearly a transitional book, Tate published five more volumes of verse—*Memoir of the Hawk* (2002), *Return to the City of White Donkeys* (2004), *The Ghost Soldiers* (2008), *Dome of the Hidden Pavilion* (2015), and posthumously *The Government Lake* (2019)—each consisting entirely of prose poems written in his now perfected narrative style. The first poem in *Memoir of the Hawk*, "New Blood," sets the nonchalant yet unsettling tone as it begins:

> A huge lizard was discovered drinking
> out of the fountain today. It was not menacing
> anyone, it was just very thirsty.

The poem goes on to say that the lizard's "long forked tongue was like a red / river hypnotizing the people, keeping them in a / trance-like state." It ends with this somewhat mysterious exchange:

> "It's like a different town,"
> one of them whispered. "Change is good," the
> other one whispered back.

Indeed, for Tate the change is good. He ropes in his wilder impulses by incorporating them into mini-stories like this, highly compressed and all the more evocative because of it. Does a poetic narrative of this sort have one sure denotative meaning? No. But it has any number of connotative meanings. For example, it can be taken to say something about how people in crowds, people in the aggregate, spontaneously adopt a group identity and behave in ways that might well embarrass them as individuals if pointed out later. There is something both sinister and amusing about this, a mixed message that Tate captures perfectly with his absurd yet threatening imagery of the giant lizard and its thirsty red tongue.

Of course that is only one reading. Many others are possible, which makes these marvelous late-period prose poems by Tate some of the richest in our literature. What brings them into being is his deft use of narrative to give shape to his widely wandering imagination. I'll leave you with one more, also from *Memoir of the Hawk*, called "Negative Employee Situation." It begins:

> The Huntingtons had a live-in maid
> by the name of Mary. Mary was very religious
> and prayed a good deal of the time.

We learn that "Mary pretty much ceased / working altogether and prayed all of the time." In fact, the mistress of the house now does all of the cooking and cleaning, but "Mr. / Huntington would never rebuke Mary because /

he believed her prayers benefited the whole / household." Then Mary dies, and the Huntingtons hire another Mary, who unfortunately doesn't seem to understand her real duties. She cleans instead of praying, with this chilling ending:

> The Huntingtons were terrified for their lives
> and discussed plans for killing the new Mary.

In keeping with the other installments in this series, I want my tribute poem to be related to a poem that I have discussed in the tribute essay. Normally the poem would be from a book I really admire. In this case, however, the James Tate poem that inspired me is from what I consider to be his period of mostly lesser work, basically his middle period. It is "Poem to Some of My Recent Poems," from the book *Constant Defender* (1983). For me, it stands out from many of the other poems in the book because the silly, self-referential conceit allows him to make a number of very witty jokes (mainly self-deprecating) and to one-up his idol Wallace Stevens in the Let's Write Another Great Poem About Poetry Sweepstakes.

Much of the poem is devoted to the demeaning yet endearing nicknames he has given his poems: "My beloved little billiard balls," "my polite mongrels," "edible patriotic plums," "my little rum runners" (again with the diminutive). He also writes of the mother of his poems (another name for the muse I think), who "had defective / tear ducts and could only weep iced tea." At one point he gives us what I believe is a tantalizing glimpse into his compositional technique, particularly in regard to endings: "I had to navigate carefully around her brain's / avalanche lest even a decent finale be forfeited." The ending, like so many of Tate's best endings, manages to be ridiculous, moving and profound all at once:

> as she was dying, I led each of you to her side,
> one by one she scorched you with her radiance.
> And she is ever with us in our acetylene leisure.
> But you are beautiful, and I, a slave to a heap of cinders.

Love Poem to My Love Poems

(after "Poem to Some of My Recent Poems" by James Tate)

Honestly, most of you are better than what you try so hard
to celebrate. Not that you have given Shakespeare's bones
any reason to quiver with envy in their dark eternal nest,
but you are manifestly superior to any song by Air Supply.
Somewhere in that amorphous vacant lot
between immortality and mediocrity
is where you little lichens cling to the cracked stone
that is my life. Some of you are phosphorescent
and glow occasionally, others pulse with a primitive beat
in the blood that is either very bad jazz
or very good rock and roll. One of you repented
and joined a speechless monastery where the only poetry
allowed is the bell tolling for the noonday meal.
Another decided to become a policeman, who when called
to a domestic dispute automatically shoots to kill
both parties as a matter of general principle.
Justifiable romanticide, they call it.
There are so many ways to go wrong in this world,
so few to go right, it's a wonder any of you turned out at all.
While I am your only father, you have many mothers,
all of them desirable at one point
and leaving something to be desired at another.
I hope you never lose touch with each other
because aside from your raggedy brothers and sisters
you are completely alone. Nobody cares
about anyone else's love or the stray
bastard utterance to which it may have given birth.

※

Afterword

The motives behind this book are simple and very selfish. I wanted first of all to have the pleasure of rereading poems I love, in particular poems that have mattered to me in my understanding as a reader and my development as a writer. I also wanted the pleasure of writing about them, talking about them, because that is the only way I can understand anything, by articulating my thoughts and feelings about it. And finally, I wanted to respond to them with verses of my own, either inspired by them or in tribute to them or in a few cases making fun of them.

Incidentally, to write a parody of a poem is not necessarily an act of contempt or even criticism (though obviously it can be those things). For me it is often more akin to teasing someone you love. It can be intimate and affectionate and funny while paying tribute to the unique voice and personality of the author. To have a voice that can readily be parodied is in itself an indication of how much a writer has accomplished.

The too-clever-by-half title of this book reflects my view of literature as a great river to which all of us contribute our few little drops. And by all of us, I mean readers too. Writers should certainly write to please themselves first. They can never be sure of pleasing anyone else. But like all artists they also desire their work to be known and appreciated, and that is not all ego. We humans have a fundamental desire to share things of beauty and moments of wonder. In a sense, the works we create, once we've created them, belong to everyone. Sometimes those things or moments can be dark or painful or even terrifying. One of the incredible aspects of art is that beauty can so often be wrought from ugly materials, which, let's be honest, are the stuff of much of our lives. Readers matter in this, a lot. Simply by enjoying and sharing a poem, for example, they help give it life.

It should be quite clear to anyone reading them that my essays about favorite poems are personal, not academic. I have no formal training, for one thing. Nor do I have a particular loyalty to any literary theories, most of which I find to be suspect if not pure balderdash, too often infected with the ideological madness of the moment. They come and go without rhyme or reason. In the end, a poem must stand on its own.

These essays do owe much to three departed writers who taught me by example how to read and think about a poem: James Dickey, Paul Carroll and Robert Bly. Of these, only Bly is fairly well remembered today as both a poet and a critic, which is nice for him but too bad for the other two.

Dickey is now best known as a novelist and screenwriter for the film *Deliverance*, adapted from his own book. He was also a passionate and insightful critic. His best reviews and essays are collected in *Babel to Byzantium* (1968). Three things distinguish his critical writing, in my view—his honesty, his depth and breadth of appreciation (though not for the Beats), and his sincere attempt to single out any positive feature of a book he otherwise hates, out of respect for the writer's trade.

Carroll does not seem to be remembered much at all these days, which is completely unfair. In the late fifties he edited *Chicago Review*, resigning in protest when the magazine's sponsor, the University of Chicago, refused to print an issue containing "obscene" work by William Burroughs and Jack Kerouac. He then founded *Big Table*, both a magazine and a publishing imprint. Among the books he launched was the highly influential anthology *The Young American Poets* (1968), where I first encountered Louise Glück, Charles Simic and James Tate, all featured in essays in this book. In addition, Carroll published the first two volumes of verse by Bill Knott. That alone would earn him a place as one of the best American poetry editors of all time.

However, the *Big Table* book that most affected me was Carroll's own *The Poem in Its Skin* (1968), a volume of essays each dedicated to exploring in depth a single poem by an American poet, such as John Ashbery, James Wright and W. S. Merwin. If it were being published today, this book would be faulted, and rightly so, for including no poets of color (such as Lucille Clifton and Etheridge Knight, to name just two obvious omissions, both of whom I made a point of including in the present volume) and only one woman. Aside from this defect which marks it as a product of its time, the book itself is timeless. In many ways the present volume, and the *Exacting Clam* column from which it is derived, are my attempt to carry on this fine tradition established by Carroll.

AFTERWORD

I recount much of Robert Bly's activity as a critic in the piece about him that is part of this volume. I want to add one thing here that didn't make it into that tribute. His epochal essay "A Wrong Turning in American Poetry" appeared in the third issue of *Choice* in 1963. The reason it didn't come as a complete shock is that he had already published an omnibus review of a number of then-contemporary volumes of poetry. That review had been slated to appear in the *Hudson Review*, which tried to censor some of Bly's more scathing appraisals. Whether or not you agree with Bly's often harsh assessments, it is to his credit that he dared to make them and relocated the piece to the second issue of *Choice* in 1962, where it appeared uncensored.

One book that he savaged was Alan Ansen's *Disorderly Houses*, which happened to be put out by Wesleyan University Press, the same house that published Bly's first collection *Silence in the Snowy Fields*. There can be little doubt, in my mind anyway, that the main reason Wesleyan never published a second volume by Bly was this review. Among other notable phrases, he declared that Ansen's book "shines like a mackerel in the moonlight." They don't write reviews like that anymore! But perhaps they should.

The undead critic who has most inspired me is poet Edward Hirsch. As well as being one of the two or three finest living poets in our language, he is, in my opinion, the best critic we have today. He writes the best poetry essays and curates the best anthologies. Of course, neither he nor Bly nor Carroll nor Dickey bears any responsibility for any failings in this book. On the other hand, I do believe that whatever virtues it may contain can be at least partly ascribed to their benign influence on a budding poet and critic. If this book in turn inspires you in any way, I will be more than repaid for my efforts.

A word about the poems that I selected to focus on in these tribute essays and tribute poems: my choices have been entirely personal and idiosyncratic. I like what I like, without apology. I did make a conscious decision to spend most of my time with twentieth century poets whose bones have not been picked over as much as those from previous centuries. Another guideline was that all the writers discussed here must be members of the Dead Poets Society. Then, too, the several generations that followed Yeats, Eliot, Pound, H. D., Williams, etc., mostly gravitated away from formal verse. That helped me find my own direction. Hence, the majority of poems analyzed and celebrated here are in free verse. This should not be taken to mean that I don't appreciate formal verse and don't sometimes enjoy writing it myself. In fact, it would not surprise me if that turned out to be the direction from which the next revolution comes.

Within all of these loose constraints I strove for as much variety as possible. I did not strive for diversity as such, because I feel that is a natural consequence of an open mind striving for variety and quality. Feel free to disagree with me on that. These tribute essays and tribute poems are meant to start discussions, not end them.

ACKNOWLEDGEMENTS

Grateful acknowledgment is made to the quarterly journal *Exacting Clam*, to its Publisher Jacob Smullyan and its Executive Editor Guillermo Stitch, and to Sagging Meniscus Press, for first publishing the tribute essays collected here, sometimes in slightly different versions. The tribute poems also appeared in the *Clam*, though several first appeared elsewhere. I thank those journals (some of them now defunct, but who isn't?) and their editors for publishing my work:

The Big Jewel: "The Canoe of Death"
Clover, a Literary Rag: "Cottonwood Seeds"
London Grip: "Another Minor Poet," "Love Poem to My Love Poems"
Lothlorien Poetry Journal: "What Borges Said"
MacQueen's Quinterly: "Crime Prevention in Wheaton, Illinois"
Paper Dragon: "Migration"

Photo credit: Scott Erskine

Kurt Luchs was born in Cheektowaga, New York, grew up in Wheaton, Illinois, and has lived and worked all over the United States, mostly in publishing and media. Currently he's based in Kalamazoo, Michigan. His first poetry publication came at age sixteen in the long-gone journal *Epos*, right next to a poem by Bukowski. He has also written comedy for television (*Politically Incorrect* with Bill Maher and the *Late Late Show* with Craig Kilborn) and radio (American Comedy Network), as well as contributing humor to the *New Yorker*, the *Onion* and *McSweeney's Internet Tendency*, among others. He is author of the poetry collections *Death Row Row Row Your Boat* (Sagging Meniscus, 2024), *Falling in the Direction of Up* (SM, 2021), and the humor collection *It's Funny Until Someone Loses an Eye (Then It's Really Funny)* (SM, 2017). His poetry chapbooks include *One of These Things Is Not Like the Other* (Finishing Line Press 2019), and *The Sound of One Hand Slapping* (SurVision Press 2022). He won a 2022 Pushcart Prize, a 2021 James Tate Poetry Prize, the 2021 Eyelands Book Award for Short Stories, and the 2019 *Atlanta Review* International Poetry Contest. He is a Contributing Editor of *Exacting Clam*.

www.ingramcontent.com/pod-product-compliance
Lightning Source LLC
Chambersburg PA
CBHW020330170426
43200CB00006B/337